Thoroughly Modern DRESDEN

◉ Quick & Easy Construction ◉ 13 Lively Quilt Projects for All Skill Levels

ANELIE BELDEN

C&T PUBLISHING

Text copyright © 2009 by Anelie Belden

Artwork copyright © 2009 by C&T Publishing, Inc.

Publisher: **Amy Marson**

Creative Director: **Gailen Runge**

Editors: **Susan Beck** and **Kesel Wilson**

Technical Editors: **Robyn Gronning** and **Teresa Stroin**

Copyeditor/Proofreader: **Wordfirm Inc.**

Cover Designer/Book Designer: **Kristen Yenche**

Production Coordinators: **Tim Manibusan** and **Zinnia Heinzmann**

Illustrator: **Wendy Mathson**

Photography by **Christina Carty-Francis** and **Diane Pedersen** of C&T Publishing, Inc., unless otherwise noted.

Published by C&T Publishing, Inc., P.O. Box 1456, Lafayette, CA 94549

Library of Congress Cataloging-in-Publication Data

Belden, Anelie

  Thoroughly modern dresden : quick & easy construction : 13 lively quilt projects for all skill levels / Anelie Belden.

    p. cm.

  Summary: "The ultimate compendium on the Dresden Plate block. With new construction techniques, the author explores all of the fan shape, color, and setting variations, and gives the reader projects of various skill levels"-- Provided by publisher.

  ISBN 978-1-57120-595-7 (paper trade : alk. paper)

  1. Patchwork--Patterns. 2. Quilting--Patterns. 3. Porcelain in art. I. Title.

  TT835.B3325 2009

  746.46'041--dc22

                    2008041960

Printed in China

10 9 8 7 6 5 4

Dedication

To my husband, Kevin Belden, whose love, support, and encouragement have helped me be the best that I can be. I thank him for indulging my quilting addiction, which enabled me to chase my dreams and make them a reality.

Also, to my three children, Joshua, Amilia, and Christopher—the love I have for each of them cannot adequately be put into words. As young children, they spent many hours at my store and at quilt shows, helping me as much as they could. I often put my motherly duties on hold to tend to the demands of my quilting career, and they were always willing to help and support me with unconditional love through it all.

Acknowledgments

First, I acknowledge my students, who have also become my friends and partners in creating this book. With each class, my teaching abilities have improved, and all of my students have contributed to my becoming the quilting instructor I am today. I thank them for their confidence in me as a teacher and for their support. Many of my students created quilts for the Gallery sections of this book and helped me in sewing samples. I so appreciate the time, expense, and creativity they each gave to their projects.

It was such a pleasure to work with the C&T staff of editors. The professionalism, expertise, support, and ability to make me instantly feel part of the C&T family made this journey exciting and possible.

I especially would like to thank Cheryl Ehlman, Chris Zeterburg, Kathy Schmidt, Peggy Parsons, and Susan Huntington for the fabulous quilting they did on the quilts. Their creativity and willingness to quilt is much appreciated. Friends and students provided so much help in making samples, binding the quilts, proofreading directions, naming the quilts, and so much more. I thank each and every one of you!

It was a pleasure to work with P&B Textiles, which contributed the fabrics for *Romancing the Reds*, page 30, and *Abendessen*, page 53. Moda Fabrics was also generous in providing fabrics for *Portugal*, page 41, and *Gypsy Summer*, page 60. Creating *Flower Power*, page 36, was so much fun using the fabrics supplied by Michael Miller. All of these companies are listed in the Resources section of this book, page 71.

Contents

Introduction

I first became interested in making a Dresden quilt when a group of my students requested it as a project for a quilt retreat. Not having made one before, I found it a challenge to come up with my own variation of the design. Thinking it was an easy block to make, we started to cut and sew using the traditional method of construction. Much to our surprise, the Dresden Plate would not lie flat on the block of fabric. We quickly realized how accurate each seam had to be to get the Dresden to lie flat.

The challenge was now how to construct the Dresden so quilters would be more successful and more creative with the design. This all led to the different Dresden designs and construction ideas for this book. I had an opportunity to present my idea to Diana McClun, quilter, teacher, and author, who thought it would make a great book and encouraged me to submit it. So here is the end result.

While researching the history of the Dresden Plate quilt design, I realized it had some possible connection to Dresden, Germany. I was born in Germany, which made this quilt pattern very personal.

My hope is that quilters are successful and enjoy the construction methods presented in this book and that they are able to express their creativity while exploring the design possibilities of this technique. It will be fun to see the creative quilts inspired by the new technique and designs presented in this book. Please see the Resources section, page 71, to send a photo of your quilt for me to see.

History of the Dresden Quilt Block

While working with the Dresden design, I became interested in learning its history. I began to research, and found it surprisingly difficult to uncover a complete story. Following is the information I did find.

The Dresden design can be seen in the earliest surviving American-made, pieced medallion quilt, labeled, "Anna Tuels Her bed quilt given to her by her mother in the year August 23, 1785." Another early example is an embroidered sampler made of white linen with needlepoint lace insertions created in Philadelphia in 1795, and known as "Dresden-work sample."

Barbara Brackman's *Encyclopedia of Pieced Quilt Patterns* contains many blocks that resemble the Dresden but have other names. A popular pattern, the Dresden typically is a full circle block. When broken to the quarter block, the name usually changes, using "Fan" within its title.

By the 1930s, the Dresden block gained popularity in the quilting world. Block 3411 in the *Encyclopedia of Pieced Quilt Patterns* is titled *Dresden Plate* and uses eight blades for the design; it was featured in the *Home Art* publication of the time. The *Kansas City Star* featured a twelve-blade block called *Dessert Plate*. Other variations used twenty blades for the design and were named *Friendship Ring* or *Friendship Circle*, *Aster*, and *Grandmothers Sunburst* or *Grandmothers Bonnet*. It became apparent that many style variations and names were associated with the Dresden block.

Dresden plates with spiraled sections and scalloped edges

The design name may have come from a town by the name of Dresden in Germany, the country where I was born. The quilt block was not designed in Germany but perhaps was inspired by the baroque art and rich porcelain designs produced there. Many of the porcelain plates had scalloped edges that resembled the Dresden design. In my mind's eye, I can see how these designs could have inspired the Dresden name.

Also made by the companies in Dresden were figurines with fragile porcelain lace. Many depicted Renaissance couples during courtship. The photograph at right shows the porcelain lace, which creates ruffle-like designs that lie so close to each other that I think they resemble the Dresden blades. These examples could have been the inspiration to name the quilt block with the curved top a Dresden.

Dresden figurine of couple playing chess.

Understanding Skill Level

For each project in this book I have indicated a skill level to give readers an idea of the ease or difficulty making the blocks will present. They are ranked as 1 for the easiest, or beginner, and 3 for the hardest, or advanced. A project that uses an advanced blade, such as the curved top, can become less difficult by replacing it with an easier blade, such as the peaked top. Of course, the opposite is true as well—a simple design can be made more challenging by substituting a level 1 blade top with a level 2 or 3 top.

When choosing tools and supplies it is most important to purchase by quality rather than by low price point. The reduced price usually indicates an inferior product made with lesser-quality materials, inferior workmanship, or suffering in accuracy.

Cutting Tools

Rotary cutting tools are far superior to scissors for cutting. They yield accurate cut edges and greatly speed the cutting process.

Rotary cutters: These tools are very sharp and need to be handled cautiously. For safety, choose a cutter that will close automatically, such as the Olfa brand. The 25mm size works well when cutting single layers of fabric and curved lines. The 45mm cutter is most commonly used.

Clear acrylic rulers: The versatile 12½″ × 12½″ size can be used to square up blocks. A 6″ × 24″ acrylic ruler is useful for cutting strips across the width of the fabric.

Cutting mat: Your cutting surface should be at least 18″ × 24.″ An optional spinning cutting mat is also helpful; it allows the mat to turn so you can cut around the templates with ease and safety.

Circle-cutting tools: Olfa's circle-cutting tool is useful for cutting perfect circles of various sizes. C&T Publishing has a rotary-cutting circle tool as does Creative Grids.

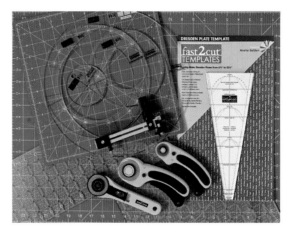

Rotary cutting tools

*Make all your Dresden projects easier! The fast2cut® Dresden Plate Template is an acrylic template for cutting **all** the blade sizes you need for **any** Dresden plate project. It eliminates the need for making cutting templates. Available from C&T Publishing; see Resources, page 71.*

Template-Making Supplies

Freezer paper, Mylar plastic, template plastic, and transparent film: Any of these can be used to make templates.

Permanent marker: Use a fine-tip permanent marker to trace the template pattern onto your chosen template material.

Compass: Use a simple "math-class" type of compass to draw circles.

Fabric-Marking Tools

Choose a marker that shows up well on the fabric and that will come out when the fabric is washed. Always test markers on fabrics.

Water-soluble marker: The blue Water Soluble Marker by Clover leaves marks that disappear when they get wet. *Caution*: Do not press or iron the mark; that can set the color into the fabric.

Pencils and chalk: Roxanne's pencil comes in white or gray; laundering may be required to remove it. Clover makes a powdered chalk marker that works wonderfully but disappears quickly. Bohin makes a chalk mechanical pencil that draws a very fine line and has strong lead. The line easily erases away.

Pressing Tools

After each seam is sewn, a crisp press keeps the piecing from becoming distorted and will prevent you from sewing seams in the wrong direction.

Iron and pressing surface: Use a hot iron on a firm pressing surface.

Finger-pressing tool: Use to press the fabric down while you are piecing the quarter blocks; many types of these wooden or plastic tools are available.

Fabric-turning tool: This tool is used to push the fabric into the peaked and curved-top shapes, creating a nice flat edge.

Bias bars: Plastic or metal pressing bars are used for Celtic design work and for making vines.

Basic Sewing Supplies

Sewing machine: Should include needle-stop down, automatic needle threader, thread cutters, and quilter's appliqué and buttonhole stitches.

Use a ¼" foot to help you sew accurate seams.

Turning tool: Use a Fast Turn tool for turning spaghetti or tubing.

Hand-sewing needles: Use a fine straw size 11 or appliqué needle size 9.

Adhesive: Use fabric glue such as Roxanne's Glue-Baste-It when attaching the blades and center circle to the block.

Thread: When piecing, I recommend using a neutral thread color that blends with the colors of your fabrics. If you're using cotton fabrics, cotton thread is the ideal choice.

Straight pins: It is important to have thin pins. Pins with glass heads are able to withstand the heat of an iron.

Lightweight interfacing: Use to make curved tops and to hold down an edge until stitched. Soft Fuse is a fusible interfacing. Do Sew is not fusible but is a good lightweight material that does not add bulk.

Design wall: This is a wall with a large piece of flannel or batting tacked to it. After completing your blocks, place the parts of the quilt on the design wall. Step away from the wall, and evaluate the quilt from a distance to see the full quilt and to assess how the color and fabric placements relate to each other.

Fabric starch: Starch, either spray or liquid, gives a crisp pressed seam and holds the seam in place. It makes the edges of the blade tops stable for appliqué.

Fabric Selection

For the projects in this book, it is better to purchase quarter-yard cuts than fat quarters because you will get more blades from a long strip. For the Dresden design to be visible, the blades should contrast with the block fabric on which they are stitched.

Each Dresden quarter has five blades, and the following combinations are helpful to remember when selecting blade fabrics.

One blade fabric: Use a medium to large print, and fussy cut each blade so the print is repeated. Striped fabrics yield a large quantity of cuts. See the full Dresden in the center of *Gypsy Summer*, page 60.

Two blade fabrics: Every other blade is a different fabric. Note that when putting quarter squares together there are two layout arrangements that create the alternating pattern. See the yellow flower in *Flower Power*, page 36.

Five blade fabrics: Each blade in the quarter square is of a different fabric. This can be repeated throughout the design, no matter how the quarter square is being used. For an example of using five fabrics for the blades, see *Abendessen*, page 53.

If you are making a continuous design and the quarter squares change direction, the fabrics will have to be altered for each square. One square will use the fabric order 1-2-3-4-5, and the square next to it will use 5-4-3-2-1. See *Romancing the Reds*, page 30, and *Portugal*, page 41.

Ten blade fabrics: Use ten fabrics to give the Dresden a scrappy look. Assign each to a position on two of the quarter squares, then alternate the quarter squares; it will appear scrappy, even though the order was planned. See the blocks of *Polka Dot Daze*, page 26.

Twenty blade fabrics: This makes each blade of the full Dresden a different fabric.

Anatomy of the Dresden Design

Dresden Parts

Blades

The blades, sometimes referred to as petals, are the individual sections that make the Dresden. Five blades are used to make a quarter Dresden block; twenty blades make a full Dresden block.

Top

The top is the widest end of the blade; it makes the outer edge of the Dresden design.

Center Circle

The center of the Dresden design is a quarter, half, three-quarter, or full circle.

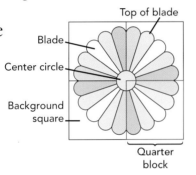

Dresden Blades

The Dresden blades can be either plain or pieced and come in three sizes: small, medium, and large. The blade size is determined by the size of block onto which the blades will be sewn. An entire quilt can be made using only one size, but sizes can also be combined as in *Flower Power*, page 36, and *Gypsy Summer*, page 60. *Blue and Yellow Sunshine*, page 19, uses a mini-blade as part of its overall design.

The blade design, along with the fabric selection, can enhance the overall look of the quilt. *Romancing the Reds*, page 30, has a vintage lace feel with the curved tops and the old-fashioned fabric prints. In contrast, *Triple Deck*, page 44, has the clean-cut lines of peaked tops and stark fabrics.

An additional variation in cutting the blades is to use two fabrics per blade as in *German Chocolate*, page 33. This creates a split in the blade and adds shading or dimension to the design.

REQUIRED TEMPLATES			
PROJECTS	**CUTTING TEMPLATES**	**PRESSING TEMPLATES**	**PLACEMENT TEMPLATES**
Blue and Yellow Sunshine	G, ZZ, D, K	MM, ZZ, DD, QQ	Large
Christmas Wreath	U, PP	DDD, PP	Christmas wreath
Polka Dot Daze	A, XX, L	AA, XX, RR	Small
Romancing the Reds	F, M, P, YY, BBB	II, SS, VV, YY	Medium
German Chocolate	F, M, P, YY	FF, SS, VV, YY	Medium
Flower Power Dresden Sampler	E, A, F, G, L, O, AAA, NN, EEE, FFF, GGG, YY, Z	EE, HH, KK, AA, UU, LL, FF, MM, HH, NN, EEE, FFF, GGG, YY, HHH	Small, medium, and large
Portugal	E, L, XX	EE, RR, XX	Small
Triple Deck	F, M	FF, SS	Medium
Amazon's Horizon	E, L	EE, RR	Small
Farfalle	E, L	EE, RR	Small
Abendessen Table Runner	E, AAA, L	HH, RR	Small
Dresden Done Royal	F, M	FF, SS	Medium
Gypsy Summer	E, G, B, M, N	KK, FF, MM, XX, SS, TT	Small, medium, and large

Dresden Blade Tops

The Dresden Plate design offers five blade-top options: straight, peaked, three-sided, curved, and 3-D half circle.

The peaked, three-sided, and curved tops all use the same template for cutting out the blade, and the construction of the blade determines the final shape of the top.

The straight top and 3-D half circle are made using the same template, with an added piece completing the top of the 3-D half-circle blade.

To determine the correct templates needed for each project, consult the Required Templates chart on page 7. Template patterns are available on the pullout.

Straight-Top Blade

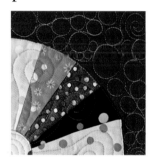

Straight top, skill level 1

The straight-top blade creates a clean line that can be used in traditional or contemporary designs. The straight-top blade is also the top blade used in making the 3-D half-circle-top blades.

Constructing the Straight-Top Blade

1. Create the cutting templates indicated on the Required Templates chart, page 7.

2. Cut strips of fabric as specified in the project's chart.

3. Place the template across the strip. Cut out the blades, alternating the direction of the blades to make the best use of the fabric.

Pressing the Straight-Top Blade

1. Trace the required pressing pattern onto the paper side of freezer paper. Iron this to 2 more layers of freezer paper, making sure the last layer has the shiny side facing out. Cut the template out.

◉ CUTTING TIP

Using a rotary cutter to cut the template keeps the lines straight and is more accurate. Designate a rotary cutter for cutting paper to keep from dulling your fabric blade.

2. Press the template onto the wrong side of the cut blades, aligning the bottom edges. The fabric blades at the top edge will be longer than the template. Use a small paintbrush to paint liquid starch onto the upper fabric edge. Fold the fabric over the template and press well.

Press straight-top blade.

Peaked-Top Blade

Peaked top, skill level 1

Resembling a sawtooth edge, the peaked-top Dresden is made up of peaks and valleys. This blade top is very versatile and can be left unstitched because it has a finished edge, or it can be stitched in place by hand or machine.

Constructing the Peaked-Top Blade

1. Create the cutting templates indicated on the Required Templates chart, page 7.

2. Cut strips of fabric as specified in the project's chart.

3. Place the template across the strip. Cut out the blades, alternating the direction of the blades to make the best use of the fabric.

4. Fold the blade in half lengthwise, right sides together, and sew across the top using a ¼″ seam. Trim the corner at the fold, and finger-press the seam open. Turn right side out.

⊙ TURNING TIP

Hold the blade with a finger in the point, then turn. Use the point of a fabric turner to make a sharp peak.

Turn peaked-top blade.

Pressing the Peaked-Top Blade

Make a pressing template by tracing the template pattern onto a piece of preshrunk muslin. Lay the stitched blade face down onto the muslin. Use your fingers to flatten the top so it is even across the top (use the template as a guide), and press.

Press peaked-top blade.

Making Split Peaked-Top Blades

Splitting the peaked-top blades in half lengthwise and using 2 fabrics to make the blade can create an additional design element (see *German Chocolate*, page 33, and *Dresden Done Royal*, page 57).

1. Take a strip of 1 fabric and sew it to a strip of a contrasting shade or color. Use a ¼″ seam, and press open. (Refer to specific project directions to determine the strip size needed.)

2. Using the appropriate cutting template, cut out the blades with the seam positioned down the center. Note: The blade must be cut with the darker fabric to the same side every time. Use caution, as it is easy to cut incorrectly.

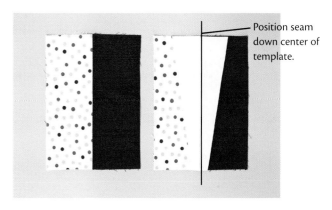

Position seam down center of template.

Cut split peaked-top blades.

3. Follow the directions in Constructing the Peaked-Top Blade, Step 4, and Pressing the Peaked-Top Blade, page 9.

○ **TIP**

Once the blade is cut, the sections of fabric that are left over can be sewn together to form another section for another blade. Note: Sew the sections together along the straight side.

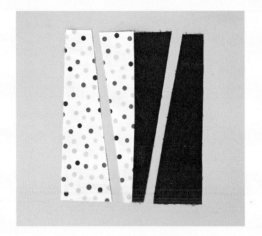

Cut split peaked-top blades from leftovers.

Three-Sided-Top Blade

Three-sided top, skill level 2

The three-sided top has the look of gears on a clock. Using a template, the 3 sides are pressed under before constructing the block. The top should be stitched down by hand or machine.

Constructing the Three-Sided-Top Blade

1. Create the cutting templates indicated on the Required Templates chart, page 7.

2. Cut strips of fabric as specified in the project's chart.

3. Place the template across the strip. Cut out the blades, alternating the direction of the blades to make the best use of the fabric.

Pressing the Three-Sided-Top Blade

1. Make a pressing template by tracing the pattern onto the paper side of freezer paper. Iron this to 2 more layers of freezer paper, being sure the last layer has the shiny side facing out. Cut out the template.

2. Press the template onto the wrong side of the cut blades, aligning the bottom edges. The fabric at the top edges will be longer than the template. Paint liquid starch onto these edges, fold down the top first, then fold the remaining sides over the template edges, and press well. Trim to ¼″ seam allowance if desired.

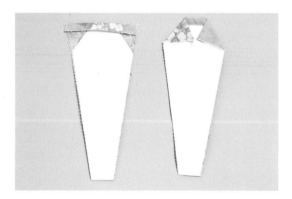

Press three-sided-top blades.

Curved-Top Blade

Curved top, skill level 3

The curved edge of the curved-top blade resembles the petals of a flower. As on the peaked blade, this blade top is completely finished during the construction process.

Constructing the Curved-Top Blade

1. Create the cutting templates indicated on the Required Templates chart, page 7.

2. Cut strips of fabric as specified in the project's chart.

3. Place the template across the strip. Cut out the blades, alternating the direction of the blades to make the best use of the fabric.

4. Create and use the indicated template to cut a facing for the curved top from Soft Fuse interfacing or Do Sew. Both are very thin, so little bulk is added. The finished blade top should be stitched down to prevent the back of the blade from showing. Although it adds bulk, fabric can be used instead of interfacing if the edges will not be stitched down

Stitching and Pressing the Curved-Top Blade

Make and use a pressing template to trace the curved edge onto the facing. Stitch carefully on the line. Trim the curve so the seam allowance is a scant ⅜″, and clip the curve. Turn the blade right side out using a fabric turner to make a smooth edge, and press.

Stitch and trim curved-top blade.

☼ FACING TIP

For *Romancing the Reds*, page 30, a thin white fabric was used for the facing of the white blades so the background fabric does not show through the blades. Instead of using a facing template to finish the rounded edge, a full template was used to cover the entire blade.

3-D Half-Circle-Top Blade

3-D half-circle top, skill level 2

The 3-D half-circle top uses additional half circles placed behind the Dresden straight-top blades and half circles added to the straight-top blades. This fun option is very effective when used for sunflowers or to make a wreath as in the *Christmas Wreath*, page 23, or *Flower Power*, page 36.

Constructing the 3-D Half-Circle-Top Blade

1. Create the cutting templates indicated on the Required Templates chart, page 7, for the half circles.

2. Layer 2 pieces of fabric with right sides together. Draw the circle onto the wrong side of 1 of the fabrics. Stitch on the drawn line.

3. Cut out the circle ⅜″ away from the sewn edge, then cut into 2 half circles. Clip the curves, and turn right side out using the fabric turner to make a smooth edge; press.

Stitch circle, and cut into halves.

Dresden Centers

The center of the Dresden design can be a quarter, half, three-quarter, or full circle. Once in place, the center circle can be secured using the stitching method of your choice (see Dresden Stitches, at right). The layer of fabric under the center circle can be trimmed away to reduce bulk.

Quarter Center Circle

Used on quarter squares, as in *Farfalle*, page 50, this can also be made as a full circle by sewing 4 together, giving the option of having 4 different fabrics in the center circle. See *Abendessen*, page 53, as an example.

Half Center Circle

A half circle of fabric can be used for the center, or 2 quarter squares can be sewn together to create a half center circle. See *Triple Deck*, page 44.

Three-Quarter Center Circle

To achieve the three-quarter center circle, use a half circle and a quarter circle. See *German Chocolate*, page 33.

Full Center Circle

Used when 4 quarter squares are sewn together to make a full square, this circle is appliquéd onto the full square. Alternatively, separate quarter circles can be sewn together to create the full circle, as in *Romancing the Reds*, page 30.

Quarter, half, three-quarter, and full center circles

Dresden Stitches

The edge stitching on the blade tops and the center circles can be sewn before the squares are stitched together **or** after the top is complete. Refer to each project to decide what will work best. Choose from the stitching techniques described below, depending on the finished look you desire.

Straight Stitch

Simple stitching with a straight stitch will hold the blade edge down. This can be sewn at the piecing stage (before quilting) or at the quilting stage. Samples of this can be seen on *Polka Dot Daze*, page 26, and *Romancing the Reds*, page 30.

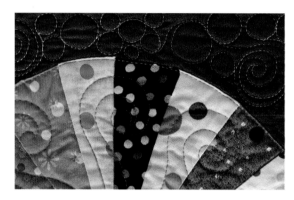

Straight-stitched edge

Decorative Buttonhole Stitch

When using this option, it is best to complete the stitching **before** quilting. It is easier to handle this process when the stitching is sewn on individual blocks, before the top is set together. The buttonhole stitch (sometimes called a blanket stitch) can be sewn by machine, if available as a preset decorative stitch. Hand stitching is also an option for those who enjoy handwork. *Blue and Yellow Sunshine*, page 19 , is an example of blades sewn with buttonhole stitching.

Buttonhole stitch by machine

Invisible Stitch

This option is used to hold down edges without any stitching showing on top of the design. Most sewing machines have a stitch (often called a blind stitch) that is inconspicuous, especially when using a clear invisible thread or a thread that matches the fabric. The key is to stitch along the side of the appliqué fabric on the background fabric, and to make the stitch small, so it is not noticeable.

Invisible stitching by machine

If you're stitching by hand, use an invisible appliqué stitch. The thread should be a single strand and should be the same color as the fabric. Use a thin hand-sewing needle, such as a size 9 straw needle, and follow the steps below for successful invisible stitching.

1. Bring the needle up from the wrong side of the background fabric, piercing the appliqué shape through the folded edge of the fabric. It is very important to be on the fold and **not** on top of the fabric; this will ensure an invisible stitch. Pull the thread up through the fabric until the knot rests on the back of the fabric.

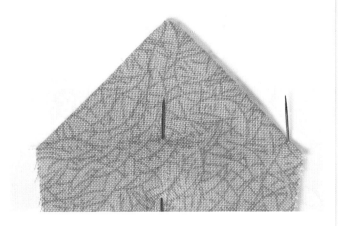

2. Pierce the needle into the background fabric right next to the folded edge of the appliqué and right next to where the thread came out of the fold of the fabric. **Do not** travel forward when piercing back into the background. This causes the thread to show, and therefore the stitch will not be invisible. Do not pull the needle and thread through yet.

3. Rock the needle up, and begin again with Step 1 by piercing the fabric through the edge of the fold of the fabric. The stitches should be about $\frac{1}{16}''$ apart.

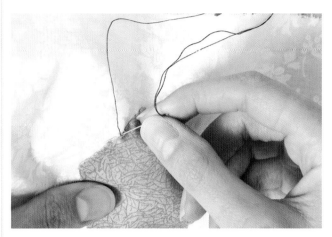

No Stitching

Some of the blade tops can be left free, adding dimension to the design. The blades that work with this method are the 3-D half circle and the peaked tops. When quilting, the edges can be stitched down (see *Christmas Wreath*, page 23).

Unstitched edges

Dresden Blocks and Designs

Making a Dresden quilt starts with choosing one or more block arrangements. The arrangement of the blocks and the interplay between them can result in a wide variety of finished quilt tops. These are categorized as full Dresden, continuous Dresden, fractured Dresden, or combination Dresden. Becoming familiar with the blocks and layouts available gives you the freedom to design your own version of a Dresden quilt.

Dresden Blocks

Quilts with Dresden designs can be made using quarter blocks, half blocks, three-quarter blocks, and full blocks.

Quarter block

Half block

Three-quarter block

Full block

Dresden Block Sizes

Three block sizes are used for the projects in this book: 6″, 9″, and 12″ finished blocks. There are also three blade sizes: small, medium, and large. The 6″ block uses the small blades, the 9″ block uses the medium blades, and the 12″ block uses the large blades.

Some of the projects can be made in other sizes (if desired), which produces another size quilt without changing the design of the top. For example, *Romancing the Reds*, page 30, is made using a 9″ (medium) block and finishes at 72½″ × 90½″; if made using a 6″ (small) block, it would finish at 48½″ × 60½″, and if made using a 12″ (large) block, it would finish at 96½″ × 120½″.

Dresden Designs

Full Dresden

The full Dresden is made of four quarter blocks that complete a circle. This can be used by itself as in *Blue and Yellow Sunshine*, page 19, *Polka Dot Daze*, page 26, and *Christmas Wreath Wallhanging*, page 23. It can also be used with other arrangements such as in *German Chocolate*, page 33, and *Romancing the Reds*, page 30.

Continuous Dresden

Connecting Dresden quarter blocks with alternating blade layouts creates a continuous design such as in *Dresden Done Royal*, page 57, *Portugal*, page 41, and *Amazon's Horizon*, page 47.

Fractured Dresden

When sewing the Dresden blocks together, any arrangement that is not a full Dresden and is made up of four quarter blocks, a three-quarter block, a half block, and/or quarter blocks is called a fractured Dresden. See *Gypsy Summer*, page 60, and *German Chocolate*, page 33, as examples.

Combination Dresden

A combination Dresden mixes full, continuous, and/or fractured arrangements in one quilt, such as in *Romancing the Reds*, page 30, and *Triple Deck*, page 44.

Preparing Quarter Blocks

Once you have cut the quarter blocks, prepare the block (before sewing the blades in place) by making several critical marks: a diagonal placement line on the right side of the fabric for placing the first blade correctly and placement lines for positioning the quarter circle, seams, and blade tops.

The Diagonal Placement Line

Marking Method 1

Place a ruler diagonally across the block. Use an erasable marking tool to draw a line from corner to corner.

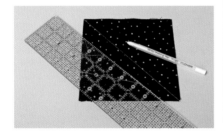

Mark diagonal placement line.

Marking Method 2

Fold the block in half diagonally, right sides together. Gently press, being careful not to stretch the bias diagonal fold. This crease will be the diagonal placement line.

Press diagonal placement line.

Placement Lines for Quarter Center Circle, Seams, and Top of Blades

The center circle placement line is used for placement of the bottom of the blades. If the blades are not placed correctly, they will not align with the edge of the block and will not match when sewn together as half and continuous Dresdens. The top of the blades and the seamlines are also marked to ensure correct alignment.

Use the placement template and an erasable tool in the following steps:

1. Mark the center circle placement line at a corner where the diagonal placement line is drawn.

2. Mark the position of the seams of each blade.

3. Mark the position of the top center of each blade.

Mark center of blade tops, seams, and quarter center circle.

Sewing Blades onto the Quarter Block

Determining the Design

Lay the blades out in the arrangement in which they will be sewn onto the quarter block, confirming the color placement. Do this for all variations. Number the blades from left to right, 1 to 5.

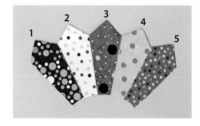

Color placement layout

○ Trial Run

Before making the first quarter block for the quilt, make a test block. This allows you to become familiar with the technique and to troubleshoot any problem areas.

Placement of the Dresden Blades

1. Fold the center blade (#3) in half lengthwise, right sides together, and press. Unfold.

2. Lay the center blade (#3) on the quarter block with the right side of the blade fabric facing up. Check the following:

    a. The diagonal placement line of the quarter block and the center fold line of the blade are aligned.

    b. The bottom of the blade is on the center circle placement line. The bottom side corners should be on the line, which makes the center of the blade cover the curve of the center circle placement line.

    c. The top of the blade matches the top markings.

3. Pin the blade in place.

Position center blade on quarter block.

Placing and Sewing the Remaining Blades

1. Lay the next blade (#4) on top of the first, with right sides facing, matching the straight edges. Sew, using a ¼″ seam, backtacking 2 stitches at the top of the blade. Once it is sewn, flip the #4 blade over and press. Check that the blade aligns with the marked placement lines.

Sew blade #4, then flip and press.

2. Repeat with the remaining blades. Blades #1 and #5 should align with the side edges of the background square.

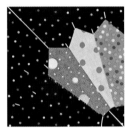

Place and sew blade #5, then flip and press.

Place and sew blade #2, then flip and press.

Place and sew blade #1, then flip and press.

Sewing 3-D Half Circles

Blades with a 3-D top start as straight-top blades and have dimension added with 3-D half circles after sewing the quarter-squares blocks together.

1. The straight blades are sewn in place as in Sewing Blades onto the Quarter Block, pages 16–17, with one slight variation. When stitching the blades onto the square, leave the top ¼″ of the seam free. This allows the 3-D half circles to be tucked under the straight blade.

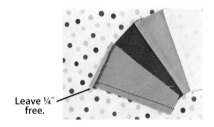

Leave ¼″ free.

Straight blades sewn in place

2. Tuck 3-D half circles under the blades about ¼″, and pin in place. (Refer to Constructing the 3-D Half-Circle-Top Blade, page 11.) The centers of the blades of this bottom layer align with the seams of the top blades. Baste using a machine basting stitch.

Position bottom layer of 3-D half circles.

3. Place the top layer of 3-D half circles on top of the bottom layer. The sides of these half circles should meet each seam of the top blades and be tucked under the blades by ¼". A tuck can be made in the half circles to make them fit. Pin in place. Topstitch along the edge of the straight top of the top blades, stitching all of the 3-D half circles in place.

Position top layer of 3-D half circles.

Sewing Center Circles

Once the blades are sewn onto the blocks, the next step is to add the center circle. First evaluate whether the center is a quarter, half, three-quarter, or full circle and evaluate the fabric that will be used for the center. The center circle can either match the Dresden design or the background it is against. If the design uses half, three-quarter, or full circles, sew the blocks together before attaching the center circles.

Sewing a Quarter Circle

1. Make a template out of the quarter-circle cutting pattern.

2. Cut out the number of quarter circles needed for the project.

3. Make a template from freezer paper of the quarter-circle pressing pattern.

4. Place the pressing template on the wrong side of the quarter-circle fabric. The straight edges of the template should align with the straight edges of

the fabric. The curved side of the fabric will extend past the template by ¼".

5. Fold the extended fabric along the curve, paint with liquid starch, and press. Once the seam has been pressed, the template can be removed and used over and over again.

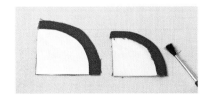

Make quarter circle.

6. Place the prepared quarter circle on the sewn block. Pin or glue it in place. Stitch using your choice of stitching (see Dresden Stitches, page 12).

Sewing a Half Circle

When 2 quarter blocks are sewn together, creating a half center circle, it is easier to make 1 half center circle than 2 quarter circles. Follow the directions for a quarter circle using the half-circle patterns for cutting and pressing.

Make half center circle.

Sewing a Three-Quarter Center Circle

The three-quarter center circle is a combination of a quarter center circle

and a half center circle. Follow the directions above for each of these to make a three-quarter center circle.

Make three-quarter center circle.

Sewing a Full Center Circle

When 4 quarter blocks are sewn together, creating a full center circle, it is easier to make a full center circle than 4 quarter circles.

1. Make a template from the full-circle pressing pattern.

2. Place the template on the wrong side of the fabric. Cut the fabric approximately ¼" larger than the template.

3. Sew a basting stitch around the edge of the fabric by hand or machine.

4. Pull on the threads of the basting stitch to gather the edge of the fabric around the template. Apply starch on the seam allowance, and press well. Remove the template.

Make full center circle.

5. Place the finished full circle on the sewn block. Pin or glue it in place. Stitch using your choice of stitching (see Dresden Stitches, page 12).

Blue and Yellow Sunshine

Pieced by Anelie Belden; quilted by Kathy Schmidt.

FINISHED QUARTER BLOCK: 13″ × 13″ | FINISHED QUILT: 37½″ × 37½″ | SKILL LEVEL 1—BEGINNER

Straight setting, three-sided-top blade, full-circle Dresden

This quilt is great for the beginner because the full-circle Dresden requires only matching the tops of the Dresden and is forgiving if the center does not match perfectly. The appliquéd vine with mini-Dresdens adds a creative border.

Fabric Requirements and Cutting

The light background is as fresh as spring and allows the bright yellows and blues in the Dresden fabrics to stand out. The blades incorporate print fabrics—2 mostly blue, 2 mostly yellow, and 1 print with yellow and blue combined.

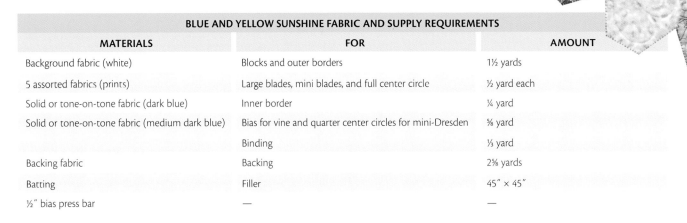

BLUE AND YELLOW SUNSHINE FABRIC AND SUPPLY REQUIREMENTS		
MATERIALS	**FOR**	**AMOUNT**
Background fabric (white)	Blocks and outer borders	1½ yards
5 assorted fabrics (prints)	Large blades, mini blades, and full center circle	½ yard each
Solid or tone-on-tone fabric (dark blue)	Inner border	¼ yard
Solid or tone-on-tone fabric (medium dark blue)	Bias for vine and quarter center circles for mini-Dresden	⅝ yard
	Binding	⅓ yard
Backing fabric	Backing	2⅝ yards
Batting	Filler	45″ × 45″
½″ bias press bar	—	—

BLUE AND YELLOW SUNSHINE CUTTING INSTRUCTIONS				
FABRIC	**FOR**	**STRIPS**	**SUBCUT**	**CIRCLES**
Background fabric (white)	Outer border	Cut 4 strips 5″ × WOF*.	Subcut 4 lengths 5″ × 28½″ and 4 squares 5″ × 5″.	—
	Blocks	Cut 2 strips 13½″ × WOF.	Subcut 4 squares 13½″ × 13½″.	
5 assorted fabrics	Large blades	Cut 1 strip from each fabric 9⅞″ × WOF.	Subcut 4 from each fabric using template G (Use pressing template MM.)	—
	Mini blades	Cut 1 strip 3″ × 12″ from each fabric.	Subcut 8 from each fabric using template D. (Use pressing template DD.)	—
	Full center circle	—	—	Cut and press 1 using template ZZ.
Dark blue fabric	Inner border	Cut 4 strips 1½″ × WOF.	Subcut 2 lengths 1½″ × 26½″ and 2 lengths 1½″ × 28½″.	—
Medium dark blue fabric	Bias for vine	Cut 8 bias strips 2″ × 16″.	—	—
	Binding	Cut 4 strips 2¼″ × WOF.	—	—
	Quarter center circles for mini-Dresden	—	—	Cut 8 using template L. (Use pressing template RR.)

* WOF = width of fabric

Making the Dresden Block

1. Determine the layout of the colors for the Dresden blades.

2. Follow the directions in Three-Sided-Top Blade, page 10, to prepare 20 of the three-sided blades.

3. Follow the directions in Preparing Quarter Blocks and Sewing Blades onto the Quarter Block, pages 16–17, to sew the blades onto the 4 quarter blocks.

4. Sew 2 of the quarter blocks together to make a half Dresden block. Make 2.

5. Sew the 2 half Dresden sections together to make a full Dresden block.

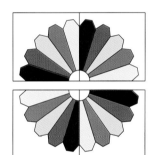

Dresden block diagram

6. Appliqué the center circle in place, using a buttonhole stitch, by machine or by hand. Note: For directions and other stitch choices, see Dresden Stitches, page 12.

Assembling the Top

Quilt assembly diagram

Inner Border

1. Sew the 26½″ borders onto opposite sides. Press the seams toward the inner border.

2. Sew the 28½″ borders onto the remaining 2 sides. Press the seams toward the inner border.

Outer Border

Mini-Dresden on Outer Border

note: *The mini-Dresdens sewn on the side borders are constructed using a different method. Instead of being sewn onto a block, the blades are stitched to each other as described below.*

1. Prepare 40 blades with peaked tops for the mini-Dresdens, using the appropriate template as directed in Peaked-Top Blade, page 9.

2. Sew 5 blades together along the side seams. Make 8 quarter Dresdens, pressing the seams to one side.

3. Appliqué the center quarter circle onto the blades by hand, using an invisible appliqué stitch.

4. Press the side seams of the pieced mini-Dresdens under ¼″. Set them aside until the vine has been made and appliquéd to the border.

Creating the Vine

The bias vines are made using the bias bar method. Use the ½" bar for pressing.

1. Fold the 2" bias in half lengthwise, with *wrong* sides together. (This may seem wrong, but it is correct.)

2. Stitch a generous ½" away from the *fold*. Stitch about 5", and then slip the ½" bias bar into the sewn section. Check to be sure the bar can slide in and out fairly easily and without stretching the fabric. Sew the remaining length of the strip. Repeat until all 8 strips are sewn. Trim the seam allowance to ¼".

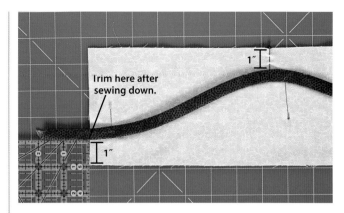

Mark vine placement.

Sew bias strips.

3. To press the bias strips, slide the bar inside, and then rotate the strip so the seam is running along the flat side of the bar. Press the seam to one side. The seam allowance should be completely under the bar. If any is extending, readjust the seam along the back, or trim the seam allowance again.

Bias Vine and Mini-Dresden Placement

1. Fold each border in half and then in quarters; press. This marks the center, which is the lowest point of the arch in the vine and is where the Dresden will be placed. It also marks the quarters, where the highest points of the arch in the vine are placed. The highest and lowest points of the vine should measure 1" from the border edges.

2. Lay the bias strips in place, gently arching as in the quilt photo on page 19. Pin or glue the vine in place. Stitch using an invisible appliqué stitch or other stitch as desired. Trim the vine ends even with the border.

3. Place the mini-Dresdens at the middle of each border, and pin into place covering the vine ends. Stitch down as desired.

4. Place a mini-Dresden on a corner of each of the 5" x 5" white squares. Pin in place. Stitch down as desired.

Attaching Borders

1. Sew the 28½" white outer borders onto opposite sides. Press the seams toward the inner border.

2. Stitch a mini-Dresden square onto each end of the remaining borders. Catch the vine ends in the seam allowance.

3. Sew the borders—with the corner squares sewn to them—to the upper and lower edges of the quilt top. Catch the vine ends in the seam allowance.

Quilting

Kathy Schmidt, a student, used a feathering design for the blades and to fill in the background squares. She quilted additional mini-blades and echoed around the vine, which carried the design through the border.

Christmas Wreath Wallhanging

Pieced and quilted by Anelie Belden.

FINISHED QUARTER BLOCK: 13″ × 13″ | FINISHED QUILT: 40½″ × 40½″ | SKILL LEVEL 1—BEGINNER

Straight setting, 3-D half-circle-top blade, full-circle Dresden

The outer edge of this holiday wreath uses the 3-D top, giving it dimension. The center area has been enlarged and the appliquéd circle omitted, allowing the background fabric to show. To add charm, the wallhanging can be decorated by adding ruching and attaching bells, buttons, or other ornamental embellishments. For easy removal, pin the embellishments in place with safety pins.

Fabric Requirements and Cutting

Select a large print for the outer border fabric, using the colors in the print to determine the remaining fabrics for the quilt. For the blades, small-print fabrics with a variety of values work well. Use the darkest green for the under layer of the 3-D tops to achieve a shadow effect. The background fabric is best if it has a high contrast to the blades so the wreath will stand out.

CHRISTMAS WREATH FABRIC AND SUPPLY REQUIREMENTS

MATERIALS	FOR	AMOUNT
Beige fabric	Background	⅞ yard
5 assorted green small-print fabrics	Blades and 3-D tops	¼ yard of each fabric
1 darkest green small-print fabric	Back layer of 3-D tops	⅛ yard
Green tone-on-tone print fabric	Inner border	¼ yard
	Binding	⅜ yard
Christmas poinsettia large-print fabric	Outer border	1 yard
Red accent fabric	Ruching and bow	⅜ yard
Backing fabric	Backing	2⅞ yards
Batting	Filler	Approximately 48″ × 48″
Buttons, bells, or small decorations	Embellishments	As desired

CHRISTMAS WREATH CUTTING INSTRUCTIONS

FABRIC	FOR	STRIPS	SUBCUT	CIRCLES
Beige fabric	Background	Cut 2 strips 13½″ × WOF*.	Subcut 4 squares 13½″ × 13½″.	—
5 assorted green small-print fabrics	Blades	Cut 1 strip from each fabric 6⅜″ × WOF.	Subcut 4 from each fabric using template U. (Use pressing template DDD.)	—
	Circles for 3-D tops	—	—	Cut and press 2 of each fabric using template PP.
1 darkest green small-print fabric	Back layer of 3-D tops	—	—	Cut and press 10 using template PP.
Green tone-on-tone print	Inner border	Cut 4 strips 1½″ × WOF.	—	—
	Binding	Cut 5 strips 2¼″ × WOF.	—	—
Poinsettia large-print	Outer border	Cut 4 strips 6½″ × WOF.	—	—
Red accent fabric	Ruching	Cut 1 strip 3″ × WOF.	—	—
	Bow	Cut 1 strip 8″ × WOF.	—	—

* WOF = width of fabric

Making the Dresden Block

1. Determine the layout of the colors for the Dresden blades.

2. Follow the directions in Straight-Top Blade, page 8, and Preparing Quarter Blocks and Sewing Blades onto the Quarter Block, pages 16–17, to prepare the straight-top blades and make 4 quarter blocks.

3. Sew 2 quarter blocks together to make a half Dresden block. Make 2.

4. Sew the 2 half Dresden sections together to make a full Dresden block.

5. Follow the directions in 3-D Half-Circle-Top Blade, page 11, to create the 3-D half circles. Follow the directions in Sewing 3-D Half Circles, page 17, to sew the 3-D-top blades onto the blocks.

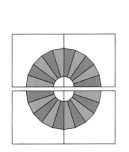 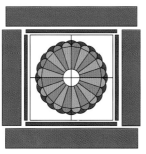

Dresden block diagram   Quilt assembly diagram

Inner and Outer Borders

Refer to Standard Borders—No-Measure Method, page 65, for sewing the borders onto the quilt.

Quilting

The background quilting is an allover design of 3-tier tear-drops. The wreath is quilted using a wavy line that starts in the middle and spirals out to the outer edge, stitching over the lines that hold down the 3-D half circles. The inner border is quilted with holly leaves, and the outer border is quilted with a wavy feathering design.

Center Circle Ruching

Unlike the other Dresden designs in this book, the center circle is not appliquéd. Instead, the raw edges of the blades are covered with ruching. The ruching should be sewn to the quilt after the quilting is completed so it is not in the way during the quilting process.

Making the Ruching

1. Take the 3″ strip cut from the ruching fabric and fold it into thirds along the length of the strip; press well. Note: Be sure the raw edge of the strip does not extend to the folded edge.

2. Hand sew a zigzag basting stitch along the strip. Pull on the threads while stitching to gather up the strip; continue to the end of the strip. Check that the strip is long enough to go around the circle, approximately 20″.

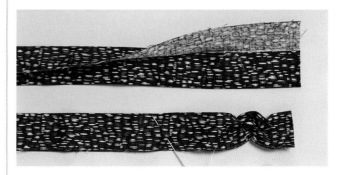

Prepare ruching strip.

3. After quilting, place the ruching over the raw edges of the blades' ends, and pin or glue in place with fabric glue. Hand stitch using an invisible appliqué stitch.

Bow

1. Cut a 3″ piece from one end of the fabric strip; this will form the knot to hold the bow. Fold this strip in half lengthwise, right sides together, and sew using a ¼″ seam allowance. Turn it right side out; press.

2. Fold the 8″ strip in half lengthwise, right sides together, and sew using a ¼″ seam allowance. Turn it right side out; press flat. Press the raw edges at each end to the inside, and stitch by hand or by machine.

3. Fold the 8″ strip in half. Fold each end toward the center to form a bow. Make the loops approximately 4½″ long on each side. Take the knot strip and wrap it around the bow. Note: The knot strip should be cut to the needed length; stitch it in the back to hold it in place. It is best to attach the bow to the wreath using a safety pin so it can be removed for cleaning or pressing.

Make bow.

Polka Dot Daze

Pieced by Anelie Belden; quilted by Kathy Schmidt.

FINISHED QUARTER BLOCK: 6″ × 6″ | FINISHED QUILT: 47½″ × 47½″ | SKILL LEVEL 1—BEGINNER

Straight setting, straight-top blade, full-circle Dresden

This quilt is great for the beginner because the full-circle Dresden requires only the aligning of the Dresden blade tops and is forgiving if the center does not match perfectly.

Fabric Requirements and Cutting

The 2 background fabrics used for the Dresden blocks are bright and have a high contrast, which gives a striking checkerboard effect. Ten different polka dot fabrics are used to make the blades, creating a scrappy look, even though it is planned.

POLKA DOT DAZE FABRIC AND SUPPLY REQUIREMENTS

MATERIALS	FOR	AMOUNT
Dark fabric (red)	Background	⅞ yard
Light fabric (yellow polka dot)	Background	⅔ yard
10 fabrics (assorted colors and polka dots)	Blades, pieced border, center circles, and floating circles	⅝ yard of each fabric
Dark polka dot fabric	Inner border	¼ yard
	Binding (cut on the bias)	¾ yard
Backing fabric	Backing	3⅛ yards
Batting	Filler	53″ × 53″

POLKA DOT DAZE CUTTING INSTRUCTIONS

FABRIC	FOR	STRIPS	SUBCUT	CIRCLES
Dark fabric (red)	Background	Cut 4 strips 6½″ × WOF*.	Subcut 20 squares 6½″ × 6½″.	—
	Quarter center circles for border corners	—	—	Cut 4 using template L. (Use pressing template RR.)
Light fabric (yellow polka dot)	Background	Cut 3 strips 6½″ × WOF.	Subcut 16 squares 6½″ × 6½″.	—
10 assorted fabrics	Blades and pieced border	Cut 3 strips from each fabric 4½″ × WOF.	Subcut 36 from each fabric using template A: 18 for the blades and 18 for the border. (Use pressing template AA for the blades.)	—
	Full center circles	—	—	Cut and press 9 using template XX.
	Floating dots	—	—	Choose sizes as desired.
Black polka dot fabric	Inner border	Cut 4 strips 1½″ × WOF.	Subcut 2 lengths 1½″ × 36½″ and 2 lengths 1½″ × 38½″.	—
	Binding	Cut bias strips 2½″ wide. Piece a strip approximately 200″ long.	—	—

* WOF = width of fabric

Making the Dresden Quarter Blocks

1. Determine the layout of the colors for the Dresden blades. Make at least 2 different quarter blocks, and use them next to each other when putting the full block together.

2. Follow the directions in Straight-Top Blade, page 8, to prepare 180 straight blades.

3. Follow the directions in Preparing Quarter Blocks and Sewing Blades onto the Quarter Block, pages 16–17, to sew the blades onto the blocks, making the following quantities:

> **20 quarter blocks** using the dark (red) background fabric. This yields 5 full Dresden blocks.

> **16 quarter blocks** using the light (yellow polka dot) background fabric. This yields 4 full Dresden blocks.

 note: *Look at the yellow polka dot blocks, page 26, to see the results of a planned scrappy look. The red blocks in the quilt are not planned but are randomly scrappy.*

Assembling the Full Dresden Blocks

1. Sew 4 quarter blocks together to make a full Dresden block. Make 5 with the dark (red) background and 4 with the light (yellow polka dot) background.

2. Appliqué the full center circles in place using an appliqué stitch of your choice.

Assembling the Top

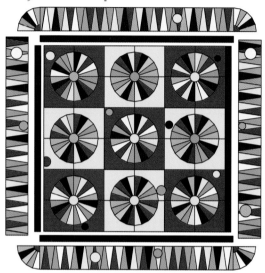

Quilt assembly diagram

1. Sew the full blocks together into rows as in the diagram. Press the seams toward the dark fabric.

2. Sew the rows together. Press.

Inner Border

1. Sew the 36½" borders onto opposite sides. Press the seams toward the inner border.

2. Sew the 38½" borders onto the remaining 2 sides. Press the seams toward the inner border.

Outer Border

1. Using blades cut from the 10 different fabrics, sew 40 together to make 1 long strip. Make 3 additional strips; press the seams in one direction.

2. Trim the last blade on each end of each long strip in half. To mark the cutting line, fold the blade in half, and cut on the fold line. This allows the ending angle to be correct for attaching the border corners.

Trim ends of pieced border.

3. Sew 2 pieced borders onto opposite sides of the quilt top.

◎ BORDER TIP

It is best to sew inner and outer borders in the same order (sides first, then upper and lower edges).

4. Before attaching the last 2 borders, construct the corners for the borders. Sew 5 blades together; press the seams to one side. When pressing, lay the sewn blades on a square to ensure the proper angle of the sides. Stitch the quarter circle to the sewn blades.

Make border corners.

5. Sew the corner Dresden blocks onto the ends of the remaining pieced borders. The corner units should match the pieced border at the edge of the quarter circle. The tops of the blades will be trimmed once the border is sewn to the quilt top.

6. Sew the pieced borders, with the corners, to the remaining 2 sides of the quilt top.

7. Using a compass and a fabric-marking tool, draw a curved line for trimming the long blades of the Dresden corners. Trim, using scissors.

Trim rounded corners on border.

Floating Polka Dots

1. Make 18 floating circles of desired sizes using the same technique for making full center circles described in Sewing a Full Center Circle, page 18.

2. Put the quilt top on a design wall, and place the floating polka dots where desired, or refer to the project photo for placement. Pin or glue them in place, and stitch, using your desired stitching technique.

Quilting

The polka dot theme was extended by using circles as the quilting motif throughout the background and border of the quilt. The center of the Dresden and the floating dots are quilted using a spiral design that is repeated on the blades.

Romancing the Reds

Pieced and quilted by Anelie Belden.

FINISHED BLOCK: 9″ × 9″ | FINISHED QUILT: 72½″ × 90½″ | SKILL LEVEL 3—ADVANCED

Straight setting, curved-top blade, combination Dresden

The difficulty in making this quilt lies in the curved-top blade. Precision sewing is needed to achieve a smooth curved top.

Fabric Requirements and Cutting

The classic red-and-white fabrication uses 6 prints that are red-on-white fabric and 5 prints that are white-on-red fabric. The use of 2 background fabrics with the red and white blades gives the quilt a lacy look. This result can be achieved by using any 2-color combination.

ROMANCING THE REDS FABRIC AND SUPPLY REQUIREMENTS

MATERIALS	FOR	AMOUNT
Dark fabric (red with white print)	Background (Block D) and full center circle	1½ yards
Light fabric (white with red print)	Background (Block B), quarter center circles, and half center circles	2¼ yards
5 fabrics (red with white print) Note: The dark background fabric and the dark inner border fabric may be used as 2 of these fabrics.	Dark blades (Blocks A, B, and C)	½ yard of each fabric
5 fabrics (white with red print) Note: The light background fabric can be used as 1 of the fabrics.	Light blades (Block D)	½ yard of each fabric
Dark fabric (red with white print)	Inner border and quarter center circles for border blocks	½ yard
	Binding	¾ yard
Light large-print toile fabric (white with red print)	Outer border, corner blocks (Block C)	2 yards
Lightweight interfacing, 36″ wide	Lining for curved tops of red blades	1 yard
White lightweight (muslin) fabric	Lining for full blade of white blades	2¼ yards
Backing fabric	Backing	5⅝ yards
Batting	Filler	80″ × 98″

ROMANCING THE REDS CUTTING INSTRUCTIONS

FABRIC	FOR	STRIPS	SUBCUT	CIRCLES
Dark fabric (red with white print)	Background (Block D)	Cut 5 strips 9½″ × WOF*.	Subcut 20 squares 9½″ × 9½″.	—
	Full center circle	—	—	Cut and press 1 using template YY.
Light fabric (white with red print)	Background (Blocks A and B)	Cut 7 strips 9½″ × WOF.	Subcut 28 squares 9½″ × 9½″.	—
	Quarter center circles	—	—	Cut 28 using template M. (Use pressing template SS.)
	Half center circles	—	—	Cut 8 using template P. (Use pressing template VV.)
5 fabrics (red with white print)	Dark blades (Blocks A, B, and C)	Cut 2 strips 7½″ × WOF from each fabric.	Subcut 32 blades from each fabric using template F. (Use pressing template II.)	—
5 fabrics (white with red print)	Light blades (Block D)	Cut 2 strips 7½″ × WOF from each fabric.	Subcut 20 blades from each fabric using template F. (Use pressing template II.)	—
Dark fabric (red with white print)	Inner border	Cut 7 strips 2″ × WOF. Piece strips together.	Subcut 2 lengths 2″ × 72½″ and 2 lengths 2″ × 54½″.	—
	Quarter center circles for border blocks	—	—	Cut 4 using template M. (Use pressing template SS.)
	Binding	Cut 9 strips 2¼″ × WOF.	—	—
Light large-print toile fabric (white with red print)	Outer border	Cut 7 strips 8″ × WOF. Piece strips together.	Subcut 2 lengths 8″ × 72½″ and 2 lengths 8″ × 54½″.	—
	Corner blocks (Block C)	Cut 1 strip 9½″.	Subcut 4 squares 9½″ × 9½″.	—
Lightweight interfacing	Lining for curved tops of red blades	Cut 16 strips 2″ × WOF.	Subcut 160 using template BBB. (Use pressing template II.)	—
Lightweight white (muslin) fabric	Lining for white blades	Cut 10 strips 7½″ × WOF.	Subcut 100 using template F. (Use pressing template II.)	—

* WOF = width of fabric

Making the Dresden Blocks

1. Determine the layout of the colors for the Dresden quarter blocks. For this continuous-design fabrication, there will be 4 layouts as listed below.

Block A: red blades on white background; 14 blocks. Eight blocks will be used on the continuous design. The remaining 6 blocks can be used as quarter blocks.

Block B: red blades on the same white background as Block A; 14 blocks. Twelve blocks will be used on the continuous design. The remaining 2 can be used as quarter blocks. The blades on these blocks should be in the reverse order of the Block A blades.

Block C: red blades on different white background; 4 blocks. Used in the corners of the border, the background fabric will be the same as the outer border. The quarter center circle will be the same as the inner border. The blades will have the same blade layout as Block A.

Block D: white blades on red background; 20 blocks will be used in the body of the quilt. They can all be made with the same blade arrangement.

Block A; make 14.

Block B; make 14.

Block C; make 4.

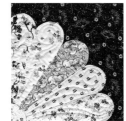
Block D; make 20.

2. Follow the directions in Curved-Top Blade, page 11, to prepare curved-top blades in the quantities and fabrications listed above. Use Do Sew curved-top facings for the red blades and muslin full-blade facings for the white blades.

3. Follow the directions in Preparing Quarter Blocks and Sewing Blades onto the Quarter Block, pages 16–17, to sew the blades onto the blocks.

4. Follow the directions in Sewing Center Circles, page 18, and refer to the assembly diagram to add the quarter center circles. Sew the blocks into horizontal rows and add the half center circles. Sew the horizontal rows together and add the full center circle.

Assembling the Top

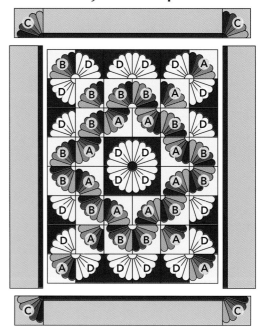
Quilt assembly diagram

Border Assembly

1. Sew the 2″ × 72½″ inner border strips to the 8″ × 72½″ outer border strips. Press toward the outer border.

2. Sew the 2″ × 54½″ inner border strips to the 8″ × 54½″ outer border strips. Press toward the outer border.

3. Sew the 72½″ border strips onto opposite sides. Press toward the inner border.

4. Sew the corner blocks to the 54½″ border strips. Sew these borders to the top and bottom. Press toward the inner border.

Quilting

The background blocks were quilted using a dense swirl design. The blades were topstitched in place, and a spiral design was stitched on each blade. The thread color matched the fabrics being quilted so the stitching would not overwhelm the print on the fabric.

German Chocolate

Pieced and quilted by Anelie Belden.

FINISHED BLOCK: 9˝ × 9˝ | FINISHED QUILT: 73½˝ × 91½˝ | SKILL LEVEL 2—INTERMEDIATE

Straight setting, split peaked-top blade, fractured Dresden

This quilt is made of quarter, three-quarter, and full Dresden blocks. The split blade and the variation of color and value give the blocks and the Dresden a dimensional look.

Fabric Requirements and Cutting

You'll need at least 5 background fabrics, ranging from light to dark in value. These fabrics may be solids or small prints. The fabrics used for the background squares can also be used as the blades. For additional interest, other fabrics can be used for the blades. When choosing the colors for the blades, refer to Special Blade-Cutting Directions, page 35. Rather than cutting and making all the blades at one time, I recommend putting the cut quarter background blocks on a design wall, then cutting the blades and placing them on the background blocks. This allows you to evaluate the arrangement before making the blades.

GERMAN CHOCOLATE FABRIC AND SUPPLY REQUIREMENTS

MATERIALS	FOR	AMOUNT
Dark fabric (dark tone-on-tone print)	Blocks (A), blades, quarter center circles, and half center circles	1⅓ yards
	Outer border	2¼ yards
	Binding	¾ yard
Medium dark fabric (tone-on-tone print)	Blocks (B), blades, quarter center circles, and half center circles	1⅛ yards
Medium fabric (tone-on-tone print)	Blocks (C), blades, quarter center circles, half center circles, and full center circle	1¼ yards
Medium light fabric (tone-on-tone print)	Blocks (D), blades, quarter center circles, and half center circles	1⅝ yards
	Inner border	½ yard
Light fabric (tone-on-tone print)	Blocks (E), blades, quarter center circles, and half center circles	1⅓ yards
Backing fabric	Backing	5⅝ yards
Batting	Filler	80″ × 99″

GERMAN CHOCOLATE CUTTING INSTRUCTIONS

FABRIC	FOR	STRIPS	SUBCUT	CIRCLES
Dark fabric (dark tone-on-tone print)	Blocks (A)	Cut 3 strips 9½″ × WOF*.	Subcut 9 squares 9½″ × 9½″.	—
	Blades	Cut 5 strips 3″ × WOF.	Piece together with another fabric, then subcut** using template F. (Use pressing template FF.)	—
	Outer border	Cut 9 strips 8½″ × WOF.	—	—
	Binding	Cut 9 strips 2¼″ × WOF.	—	—
Medium dark fabric (tone-on-tone print)	Blocks (B)	Cut 2 strips 9½″ × WOF.	Subcut 8 squares 9½″ × 9½″.	—
	Blades	Cut 5 strips 3″ × WOF.	Piece together with another fabric, then subcut** using template F. (Use pressing template FF.)	—
Medium fabric (tone-on-tone print)	Blocks (C)	Cut 2 strips 9½″ × WOF.	Subcut 8 squares 9½″ × 9½″.	—
	Blades	Cut 5 strips 3″ × WOF.	Piece together with another fabric, then subcut** using template F. (Use pressing template FF.)	—
Medium light fabric (tone-on-tone print)	Blocks (D)	Cut 4 strips 9½″ × WOF.	Subcut 13 squares 9½″ × 9½″.	—
	Blades	Cut 5 strips 3″ × WOF.	Piece together with another fabric, then subcut** using template F. (Use pressing template FF.)	—
	Inner border	Cut 7 strips 2″ × WOF.	—	
Light fabric (tone-on-tone print)	Blocks (E)	Cut 3 strips 9½″ × WOF.	Subcut 10 squares 9½″ × 9½″.	—
	Blades	Cut 5 strips 3″ × WOF.	Piece together with another fabric, then subcut** using template F. (Use pressing template FF.)	—
Fabrics of your choice	Quarter center circles	—	—	Cut using template M. (Use pressing template SS.)
	Half center circles	—	—	Cut using template P. (Use pressing template VV.)
	Full center circles	—	—	Cut using template YY.

* WOF = width of fabric
** Subcut a total of 240 blades.

○ *Special Blade-Cutting Directions*

Cutting 5 strips from each fabric (as the cutting chart indicates) may be more than the quilt will require, depending on the arrangement you decide to use. If you're cutting strips for each specific square, use the following to help determine the number of strips needed:

Quarter square (corners of the quilt): the strip length is 24″.

Half square (squares at the sides of the quilt): the strip length is 38″ or the width of the fabric.

Three-quarter squares (most of the squares in the quilt): the strip lengths are 1 at 24″ and 1 at 38″ or the width of the fabric.

Whole square in the center of the quilt: the strip length is 38″ or the width of the fabric. You'll need 2 strips.

Making the Dresden Blocks
Sewing the Split Blades

Each block has a different fabrication, determined during the cutting and design stage, as mentioned above. Refer to the diagram, at right, and the quilt photo, page 33, to judge where to place the fabrics. Begin by creating the split peaked blades.

Use the 3″ strips of dark fabric and a lighter fabric of the same color to make split peaked-top blades following the directions in Peaked-Top Blade, page 9.

Sewing Blades onto the Quarter Blocks

1. Determine the layout of the colors for each Dresden quarter block.

2. Follow the directions in Preparing Quarter Blocks and Sewing Blades onto the Quarter Block, pages 16–17, to sew the blades onto the blocks.

3. Evaluate the center circles, and decide which fabric will be used. Also, decide where quarter, half, and full center circles will be. Prepare the quarter, half, and full center circles according to the directions in Sewing Center Circles, page 18.

4. Appliqué the quarter center circles onto the squares, and stitch the tops of the blades in place using the stitching method of your choice.

Assembling the Top

Quilt assembly diagram

1. Use a design wall to lay the quilt out as in the quilt assembly diagram.

2. Sew each row together, pressing the seams in opposite directions. Appliqué the half center circles.

3. Sew the rows to each other, pinning at seam intersections to ensure that they are aligned. Appliqué the full center circles.

Inner and Outer Borders

Refer to Mitered Border Corners, page 65, for sewing the borders onto the quilt.

Quilting

The background of each square was quilted using a dense allover design. Each block has a different design quilted on it. The blades were quilted at the sides and down the center seam. The center circles were quilted with a spiral design or an allover design.

Pieced and quilted by Anelie Belden.

FINISHED QUARTER BLOCKS: 6″ × 6″; 9″ × 9″; 12″ × 12″ | FINISHED QUILT: 48½″ × 54½″

SKILL LEVEL 3—ADVANCED 💎

Straight setting, all the blade top variations, fractured and full Dresden

Making this quilt top is a wonderful way to try each of the blade-top variations without committing to one for an entire quilt.

Fabric Requirements and Cutting

Start by choosing a large floral print for the border. From this, pull the colors for the body of the quilt. Although the sample is made using bright colors and black, it can be effective using a variety of color options and flower styles.

FLOWER POWER FABRIC AND SUPPLY REQUIREMENTS		
MATERIALS	**FOR**	**AMOUNT**
Background fabric (dark)	Blocks	1¾ yards
20 assorted fabrics (variety of prints and colors)	Dresden blades and center circles	¼ to ½ yard of each fabric
Medium to large multicolored print	Border	⅞ yard
	Binding	½ yard
Backing fabric	Backing	3⅛ yards
Batting	Filler	56″ × 62″
Lightweight interfacing, 36″ wide	Curved-top blades	¼ yard
Rick rack	Trim around flower centers	2 yards

FLOWER POWER CUTTING INSTRUCTIONS					
FABRIC		**FOR**	**STRIPS**	**SUBCUT**	**CIRCLES**
Dark background fabric		Blocks A, B, C, D, E, F	Cut 5 strips 6½″ × WOF*.	Subcut 28 squares 6½″ × 6½″.	—
		Block G	Cut 1 strip 9½″ × WOF.	Subcut 4 squares 9½″ × 9½″.	—
		Block H	Cut 1 strip 12½″ × WOF.	Subcut 3 squares 12½″ × 12½″.	—
20 assorted fabrics:	All 1 fabric for Block A	Blades	Cut 1 strip 5¼″ × 33″.	Subcut 20 using template E. (Use pressing templates EE and HH.)	—
		Full center circle	—	—	Cut and press 1 using template GGG.
	5 different fabrics for Block B	Blades	Cut 1 strip 5¼″ × 8″ from each fabric.	Subcut 4 from each fabric using template E. (Use pressing template KK.)	—
		Full center circle	—	—	Cut and press 1 using template EEE.
	5 different fabrics for Block C	Blades	Cut 1 strip 5¼″ × 8″ from each fabric.	Subcut 4 from each fabric using template E. (Use pressing template HH.)	—
		Full center circle	—	—	Cut and press 1 using template YY.
	2 different fabrics for Block D	Blades	Cut 1 strip 5¼″ × 14″ from each fabric.	Subcut 7 from 1 fabric and 8 from the other using template E. (Use pressing template EE.)	—
		Full center circle	—	—	Cut and press 1 full circle using template EEE.
	5 different fabrics for Block E	Blades	Cut 1 strip 4½″ × 4″ from each fabric.	Subcut 2 from each fabric using template A. (Use pressing template AA.)	—
		Half center circle	—	—	Cut 1 using template O. (Use pressing template UU.)

FABRIC		FOR	STRIPS	SUBCUT	CIRCLES
20 assorted fabrics (continued)	2 different fabrics for Block F	Blades	Cut 1 strip 4½″ × 16″ from each fabric.	Subcut 10 from each fabric using template A. (Use pressing template AA.)	—
		Full center circle	—	—	Cut 1 using template XX.
		Circles for 3-D tops	Cut 1 strip 2″ × 12″ from each fabric.	—	Subcut and press 5 from each fabric using template NN.
	3rd fabric for Block F	Background 3-D blades	Cut 1 strip 2″ × 22″.	—	Cut 10 using template NN.
	2 different fabrics for Block G	Blades	Cut 2 strips 3″ × WOF from each fabric.	Piece strips together, then subcut 20 using template F. (Use pressing template FF.)	—
		Full center circle	—	—	Cut and press 1 using template GGG.
	5 different fabrics for Block H	Blades	Cut 1 strip 9⅞″ × 17″ from each fabric.	Subcut 3 from each fabric using template G. (Use pressing template MM.)	—
		Full center circle	—	—	Cut and press 1 using template FFF.
	Assorted green fabrics	Leaves	—	Cut 4 using template Z. (Use pressing template HHH.)	—
Medium to large multi-colored print		Outer border	Cut 4 strips 6½″ × WOF.	Subcut 1 length 6½″ × 12½″, 1 length 6½″ × 24½″, 2 lengths 6½″ × 30½″, and 1 length 6½″ × 42½″.	—
		Binding	Cut 6 strips 2¼″ × WOF.	—	—
Lightweight interfacing		Lining for curved tops, Block A	Cut 1 strip 1½″ × WOF.	Subcut 10 using template AAA. (Use pressing template HH.)	—
		Lining for curved tops, Block C	Cut 2 strips 1½″ × WOF.	Subcut 20 using template AAA. (Use pressing template HH.)	—

* WOF = width of fabric

◎ CUTTING TIP

Rather than cutting all of the fabrics at once, cut as you go. This allows flexibility in placing fabrics and developing the overall design. Cut and place fabric on a design wall to decide the color choices that work best.

Making the Dresden Blades

Make the following blades in the numbers directed for the various blocks. Refer to Dresden Blade Tops, page 8, for blade construction directions.

6″ Blocks

A: One full Dresden alternating curved-top and peaked-top blades from the same fabric; make 10 of each blade for a total of 20 blades.

B: One full Dresden using the three-sided-top blade and 5 fabrics in shades of one color; make 4 blades in each shade, for a total of 20 blades.

C: One full Dresden using the curved-top blade and 5 fabrics; make 4 blades in each fabric, for a total of 20 blades.

D: One three-quarter Dresden using the peaked-top blade and 2 fabrics in shades of one color; make 7 blades in one shade and 8 in the other for a total of 15 blades.

E: One half Dresden using the straight-top blade and 5 fabrics; make 2 blades in each fabric for a total of 10 blades.

F: One full Dresden using 3-D blades and 3 fabrics; make 10 straight-top blades in each of 2 fabrics for a total of 20 blades. Make the background half circle from the third fabric.

9″ Block

G: Make 1 full Dresden using the split peaked-top blade and 2 fabrics; make 20 blades.

12″ Block

H: Make 1 three-quarter Dresden using the three-sided-top blade with 5 different fabrics and colors; make 3 blades in each color for a total of 15 blades.

Making the Dresden Blocks

Refer to Preparing Quarter Blocks and Sewing Blades onto the Quarter Block, pages 16–17, for directions on sewing the blades onto the blocks. Most of the center circles are appliquéd in place once the top has been pieced together. Use sizes that work best with your fabrics and design.

Assembling the Top

Quilt assembly diagram

1. Using a design wall, lay the quilt out as in the quilt assembly diagram.

2. Referring to the diagram, sew each section together. Note: The border sections are incorporated while piecing the top together. Add the half center circle for Block E. Refer to Sewing a Half Circle, page 18.

3. Sew the sections to each other, pinning at seam intersections to ensure that they are aligned. Add the full center circles. Refer to Sewing a Full Center Circle, page 18.

Appliqué

Use your preferred method to appliqué 4 leaves and 2 fussy-cut flowers. Refer to the quilt photo, page 36, for placement.

Quilting

The quilting of *Flower Power* adds another dimension to its allover design. Couching of yarns, using the Bernina free-motion couching foot, can be seen in the leaves and flowers. Threads in a variety of colors were used to add design elements around flowers and more flowers in the background.

Embellishing

If you're applying embellishments to the quilt top, it is best to do this after the quilt has been quilted, since ruching, rickrack, buttons, beads, crystals, and so forth can be difficult to stitch around. Some sewing machines have a variety of decorative stitches that you can also use for embellishing by incorporating variegated, multicolored, or metallic threads.

✦ CUTAWAY TIP

After sewing a quarter, half, or full center circle in place, cut away the background fabric under the circles to remove bulk.

Gallery of Quilts with Straight Settings

Trodden Path; 61½″ × 61½″;
peaked-top blade, small block
Pieced and quilted by Anelie Belden.

Susan's Quilt; 82″ × 94″;
peaked-top blade, small block
Pieced and hand quilted by Ellen Dambacher.

Sunny Day Table Runner;
17″ × 52″;
peaked-top blade, small block
Pieced and quilted by Tammy Martin.

China Blue; 44″ × 44″;
peaked-top blade, medium block
Pieced by Ginny Hegg; quilted by Anelie Belden.

Luisita; 71″ × 71″;
peaked-top blade, small block
Pieced by Barbara J. Heard;
quilted by Kathy Schmidt.

Portugal

Pieced by Anelie Belden; quilted by Cheryl Ehlman.

FINISHED QUARTER BLOCK: 6″ × 6″ | FINISHED QUILT: 77″ × 77″ | SKILL LEVEL 2—INTERMEDIATE

On-point setting, peaked-top blade, continuous Dresden

The continuous arrangement of this Dresden design requires alternating blocks in 2 color layouts. It is important to keep them in order so the same fabrics do not end up next to each other. Frequently referring to the quilt assembly diagram and working on a design wall will help as you put this quilt top together.

Fabric Requirements and Cutting

The background is made up of a variety of yellow and golden yellow fabrics that are small tone-on-tone prints, giving the background texture and interest. Each ring of blades reads as 1 color (blue, rose, or green) although each ring is made of 5 different prints in the color range.

PORTUGAL FABRIC AND SUPPLY REQUIREMENTS

MATERIALS	FOR	AMOUNT
Main fabric (6 fabrics in variety of yellow and golden yellow prints)	Background blocks and quarter center circles	1⅛ yards of each fabric
Triangle fabric (1 golden yellow print chosen from the 6 main fabrics)	Side setting triangles and corner triangles	1 yard
5 assorted fabrics (blue for Blocks A and B)	Blades on outer ring of blocks, center Dresden blocks, and full center circle	½ yard of each fabric
5 assorted fabrics (rose for Blocks C and D)	Blades on middle ring of blocks	⅓ yard of each fabric
	Binding	⅝ yard of 1 fabric
5 assorted fabrics (green for Blocks E and F)	Blades on inner ring of blocks	¼ yard of each fabric
Backing fabric	Backing	5½ yards
Batting	Filler	85″ × 85″

PORTUGAL CUTTING INSTRUCTIONS

FABRIC	FOR	STRIPS	SUBCUT	CIRCLES
6 main fabrics (variety of yellow and golden yellow prints)	Background blocks	Cut 4 strips 6½″ × WOF* from each fabric to total 24 strips.	Subcut 144 squares 6½″ × 6½″.	—
	Quarter center circles	Cut 5 strips 1½″ × WOF.	—	Cut 108 using template L. (Use pressing template RR.)
Golden yellow fabric (chosen from 6 main fabrics)	Side setting triangles	Cut 2 strips 9¾″ × WOF.	Subcut 7 squares 9¾″ × 9¾″. Cut again into triangles by cutting diagonally twice. Yields 28 triangles.	—
	Corner triangles	Cut 1 strip 9⅜″ × WOF.	Subcut 2 squares 9⅜″ × 9⅜″. Cut again into triangles by cutting diagonally once. Yields 4 triangles.	—
5 assorted blue fabrics (Blocks A and B)	Blades on outer ring of blocks and center Dresden	Cut 3 strips 5¼″ × WOF from each fabric.	Subcut 64 blades from each fabric using template E. (Use pressing template EE.)	—
	Full center circle	—	—	Cut and press 1 using template XX.
5 assorted rose fabrics (Blocks C and D)	Blades on middle ring of blocks	Cut 2 strips 5¼″ × WOF from each fabric.	Subcut 36 blades from each fabric using template E. (Use pressing template EE.)	—
	Binding	Cut 9 strips 2¼″ × WOF from 1 fabric.	—	—
5 assorted green fabrics (Blocks E and F)	Blades on inner ring of blocks	Cut 1 strip 5¼″ × WOF from each fabric.	Subcut 12 blades from each fabric using template E. (Use pressing template EE.)	—

* WOF = width of fabric

Making the Dresden Blocks

Blocks with Blue Blades

This pattern requires 2 different Dresden quarter-block fabrications for the continuous design. The blocks are made using the background fabric for the quarter center circle.

Block A: Make 32 quarter blocks for the continuous design and the full Dresden in the center of the quilt.

Block B: Make 32 quarter blocks for the continuous design.

Block A; make 32.   Block B; make 32.

Blocks with Rose Blades

The continuous design in this fabrication also requires 2 different Dresden quarter blocks. The blocks are made using the background fabric for the quarter center circle.

Block C: Make 20 quarter blocks for the continuous design.

Block D: Make 16 quarter blocks for the continuous design.

Block C; make 20.   Block D; make 16.

Blocks with Green Blades

For this fabrication there are again 2 different Dresden quarter-block layouts required for the continuous design. The blocks are made using the background fabric for the quarter center circle.

Block E: Make 4 quarter blocks for the continuous design.

Block F: Make 8 quarter blocks for the continuous design.

Block E; make 4.   Block F; make 8.

Sewing the Blocks

1. Follow the directions in Peaked-Top Blade, page 9, to prepare the peaked-top blades.

2. Follow the directions in Preparing Quarter Blocks and Sewing Blades onto the Quarter Block, pages 16–17, to sew the blades onto the blocks.

3. Make the quarter center circles following directions in Sewing a Quarter Circle, page 18.

4. Appliqué the quarter center circles in place using the stitch of your choice. Refer to Dresden Stitches, page 12.

Assembling the Top

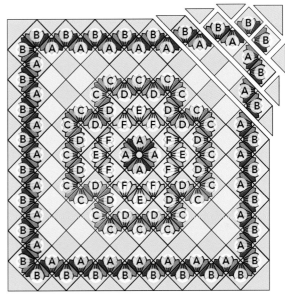

Quilt assembly diagram

1. Refer to the diagram, and sew the blocks and triangles together as diagonal rows. Press the seams for each row in opposite directions.

2. Sew the rows together. Press the seams as desired.

3. Appliqué the full center circle in place using the stitch of your choice.

Quilting

The background has been densely quilted using an allover design of flowers, leaves, and hearts. In the larger corner background area, a floral design was quilted using rose thread to add interest. The blades are not quilted as densely.

Triple Deck

Pieced by Anelie Belden; quilted by Susan Huntington.

FINISHED QUARTER BLOCK: 9″ × 9″ | FINISHED QUILT: 64½″ × 77¼″ | SKILL LEVEL 1—BEGINNER

On-point setting, peaked-top blade, fractured and continuous Dresden

The center continuous design is framed with red quarter and half Dresden blocks. The quilt becomes a rectangle by adding the final rows of black quarter Dresden blocks.

Fabric Requirements and Cutting

The striking combination of red, white, and black makes this quilt a classic. Any 3-color combination can be used for this quilt, such as red, white, and blue; blue, yellow, and green; green, burgundy, and cream; and so forth.

TRIPLE DECK FABRIC AND SUPPLY REQUIREMENTS		
MATERIALS	**FOR**	**AMOUNT**
Light background fabric (white with black print)	Background squares and quarter center circles	2⅓ yards
Dark background fabric (black solid)	Side setting triangles and corner triangles	1 yard
5 dark fabrics (black print)	Blades and quarter center circles (Blocks A, B, and C)	⅝ yard of each fabric
5 medium fabrics (red print)	Blades and quarter center circles (Block D)	¼ yard of each fabric
Medium fabric (red print)	Inner border	⅓ yard
Dark fabric (black print)	Outer border	1⅓ yards
	Binding	⅝ yard
Backing fabric	Backing	4⅞ yards
Batting	Filler	72″ × 85″

TRIPLE DECK CUTTING INSTRUCTIONS				
FABRIC	**FOR**	**STRIPS**	**SUBCUT**	**CIRCLES**
Light background fabric (white with black print)	Background squares	Cut 8 strips 9½″ × WOF*.	Subcut 32 squares 9½″ × 9½″.	—
	Quarter center circles (Blocks A and B)	—	—	Cut 12 using template M. (Use pressing template SS.)
Dark background fabric (black solid)	Side setting triangles	Cut 2 strips 14″ × WOF.	Subcut 4 squares 14″ × 14″. Cut again into triangles by cutting twice diagonally. Yields 16 triangles (2 extra).	—
	Corner triangles	—	Cut 2 squares 7¼″ × 7¼″. Cut again into triangles by cutting diagonally once. Yields 4 triangles.	—
5 dark fabrics (black print)	Blades (Blocks A, B, and C)	Cut 2 strips from each fabric 7½″ × WOF.	Subcut 20 from each fabric using template F. (Use pressing template FF.)	—
	Quarter center circles (Block D)	—	—	Cut 12 using template M. (Use pressing template SS.)
5 medium fabrics (red print)	Blades (Block D)	Cut 1 strip from each fabric 7½″ × WOF.	Subcut 12 from each fabric using template F. (Use pressing template FF.)	—
	Quarter center circles (Block C)	—	—	Cut 8 using template M. (Use pressing template SS.)
Medium fabric (red print) Note: May be 1 of the 5 red blade fabrics.	Inner border	Cut 6 strips 1½″ × WOF.	—	—
Dark fabric (black print) Note: May be 1 of the 5 dark blade fabrics.	Outer border	Cut 7 strips 6″ × WOF.	—	—
	Binding	Cut 8 strips 2¼″ × WOF.	—	—

* WOF = width of fabric

Making the Dresden Blocks

Blocks with White Background and Black Blades

For this fabrication, there will be 3 Dresden quarter-block layouts. The continuous design requires 2 blade layouts, and the outer blocks are made using different quarter center circle fabrics.

Block A: Make 8 quarter blocks for the continuous design. Use the background fabric for the quarter center circle.

Block B: Make 4 quarter blocks for the continuous design. Use the background fabric for the quarter center circle.

Block C: Make 8 quarter blocks with red quarter center circles. These are used for the top and bottom row.

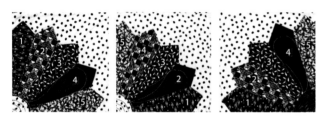

Block A; make 8.   Block B; make 4.   Block C; make 8.

Blocks with White Background and Red Blades

For this fabrication there will be 1 Dresden quarter-block layout.

Block D: Make 12 quarter blocks with black quarter center circles.

Block D; make 12.

Sewing the Blocks

1. Follow the directions in Peaked-Top Blade, page 9, to prepare the peaked-top blades.

2. Follow the directions in Preparing Quarter Blocks and Sewing Blades onto the Quarter Block, pages 16–17, to sew the blades onto the blocks.

3. Make the quarter center circles following the directions in Sewing a Quarter Circle, page 18.

4. Appliqué the quarter center circles in place using the stitch of your choice. Refer to Dresden Stitches, page 12.

Assembling the Top

Quilt assembly diagram

1. Refer to the diagram, and sew the blocks together as diagonal rows. Press the seams for each row in opposite directions.

2. Sew the rows together. Press the seams as desired.

Inner Border and Outer Borders

Refer to Standard Borders—No-Measure Method, page 65, for measuring and sewing borders.

Quilting

The use of red thread on the black background adds a striking finishing touch to this quilt. The loopy design fills the blades and is repeated on the outside border.

Amazon's Horizon

Pieced by Anelie Belden; quilted by Peggy Parsons.

FINISHED QUARTER BLOCK: 6″ × 6″ | **FINISHED QUILT:** 72″ × 80½″ | **SKILL LEVEL 2—INTERMEDIATE**

On-point setting, peaked-top blade, continuous Dresden

This quilt is made up of 3 rings of blades floating on 3 different background fabrics. The outer border can change in size to accommodate the desired finished size.

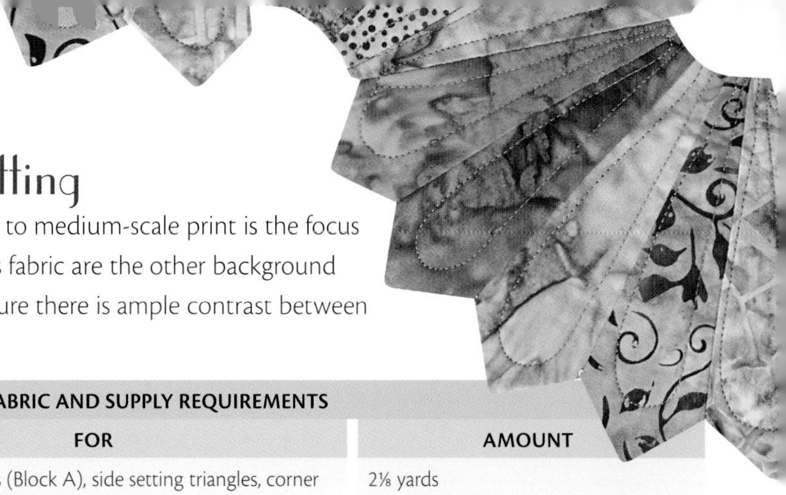

Fabric Requirements and Cutting

This quilt was made of batiks in rich, earthy tones. A large- to medium-scale print is the focus fabric on the outer edge. Two darker colors from the focus fabric are the other background fabrics, and the blades are a variety of light shades. Make sure there is ample contrast between the blades and the background fabrics.

AMAZON'S HORIZON FABRIC AND SUPPLY REQUIREMENTS		
MATERIALS	**FOR**	**AMOUNT**
Main fabric (medium to large multicolor print)	Outer edge blocks (Block A), side setting triangles, corner triangles, and quarter center circles	2⅛ yards
	Border	1⅝ yards
	Binding	⅝ yard
Dark fabric (black tone-on-tone)	Middle ring of blocks (Block B) and quarter center circles	1½ yards
Accent fabric (burgundy tone-on-tone)	Center blocks (Block C) and quarter center circles	1 yard
5 assorted fabrics (light)	Blades on outer edge blocks (Block A)	½ yard of each fabric
5 assorted fabrics (light)	Blades on middle ring of blocks (Block B)	½ yard of each fabric
5 assorted fabrics (light)	Blades on center blocks (Block C)	¼ yard of each fabric
Backing fabric	Backing	5 yards
Batting	Filler	80″ × 88″

AMAZON'S HORIZON CUTTING INSTRUCTIONS				
FABRIC	**FOR**	**STRIPS**	**SUBCUT**	**CIRCLES**
Main fabric (medium to large multicolor print)	Outer edge blocks (Block A and plain blocks)	Cut 6 strips 6½″ × WOF*.	Subcut 34 squares 6½″ × 6½″.	—
	Side setting triangles	Cut 2 strips 9¾″ × WOF.	Subcut 6 squares 9¾″ × 9¾″. Cut again into triangles by cutting diagonally twice. Yields 24 triangles (2 extra).	—
	Corner triangles	Cut 1 strip 9⅜″ × WOF.	Subcut 2 squares 9⅜″ × 9⅜″. Cut again into triangles by cutting diagonally once. Yields 4 triangles.	—
	Quarter center circles	Cut 2 strips 1½″ × WOF.	—	Subcut 22 using template L. (Use pressing template RR.)
	Border	Cut 8 strips 6½″ × WOF.	—	—
	Binding	Cut 9 strips 2¼″ × WOF.	—	—
Dark fabric (black tone-on-tone)	Middle ring of blocks (Block B)	Cut 7 strips 6½″ × WOF.	Subcut 40 squares 6½″ × 6½″.	—
	Quarter center circles	Cut 2 strips 1½″ × WOF.	—	Subcut 40 using template L. (Use pressing template RR.)
Accent fabric (burgundy tone-on-tone)	Center blocks (Block C)	Cut 4 strips 6½″ × WOF.	Subcut 23 squares 6½″ × 6½″.	—
	Quarter center circles	Cut 1 strip 1½″ × WOF.	—	Subcut 26 using template L. (Use pressing template RR.)
5 assorted fabrics	Blades on outer edge blocks (Block A)	Cut 2 strips from each fabric 5¼″ × WOF.	Subcut 26 blades from each fabric using template E. (Use pressing template EE.)	—
5 assorted fabrics	Blades on middle ring of blocks (Block B)	Cut 2 strips from each fabric 5¼″ × WOF.	Subcut 40 blades from each fabric using template E. (Use pressing template EE.)	—
5 assorted fabrics	Blades on center blocks (Block C)	Cut 1 strip from each fabric 5¼″ × WOF.	Subcut 22 blades from each fabric using template E. (Use pressing template EE.)	—

* WOF = width of fabric

Making the Dresden Blocks

1. Determine the layout of the colors for each of the 3 colorations for the Dresden blades. The blades are a scrappy unplanned fabrication.

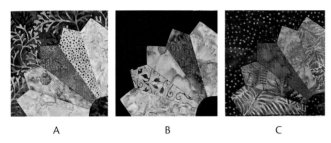

A   B   C

Color layout for quarter blocks: print background (Block A), black background (Block B), and burgundy background (Block C)

2. Follow the directions in Peaked-Top Blade, page 9, to prepare the peaked-top blades in the following quantities:

Block A: 130 blades total

Block B: 200 blades total

Block C: 110 blades total

3. Follow the directions in Preparing Quarter Blocks and Sewing Blades onto the Quarter Block, pages 16–17, to sew the blades onto the blocks, making the following quantities:

Block A: 26 print-background quarter squares

Block B: 40 black-background quarter squares

Block C: 22 burgundy-background quarter squares

4. Make the quarter center circles following the directions in Sewing a Quarter Circle, page 18.

5. Appliqué the quarter center circles in place using the stitch of your choice. Note that the quarter center circles should be the same fabric as the background area they will adjoin once the blocks are sewn together. Block A will all have black quarter circles, Block B will have 22 print and 18 burgundy quarter center circles, and Block C will have 14 black and 8 burgundy quarter center circles.

Quarter center circles should match adjoining background.

Assembling the Top

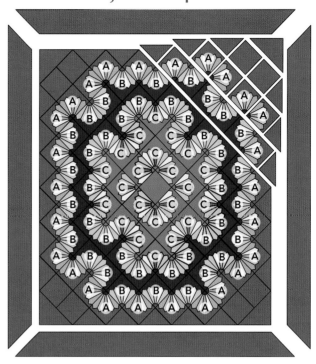

Quilt assembly diagram

1. Refer to the diagram, and sew the blocks together as diagonal rows. Press the seams for each row in opposite directions.

2. Sew the rows together. Press the seams as desired.

Borders

Refer to Mitered Border Corners, page 65, for measuring and sewing borders.

Quilting

Each blade was stitched with a simple arch at the top and straight stitching along each side. The background was quilted in an allover dense design.

Farfalle

Pieced by Anelie Belden; quilted by Peggy Parsons.

FINISHED QUARTER BLOCK: 6″ × 6″ | FINISHED QUILT: 69½″ × 86½″ | SKILL LEVEL 1—BEGINNER

On-point setting, peaked-top blade, fractured Dresden

Inspired by farfalle, commonly known as "bow-tie" pasta, the quarter squares of this design are set on point. This allows the Farfalle design to "float" in the center of the quilt. This layout is a great project for a new quilter because one Dresden block does not have to match another.

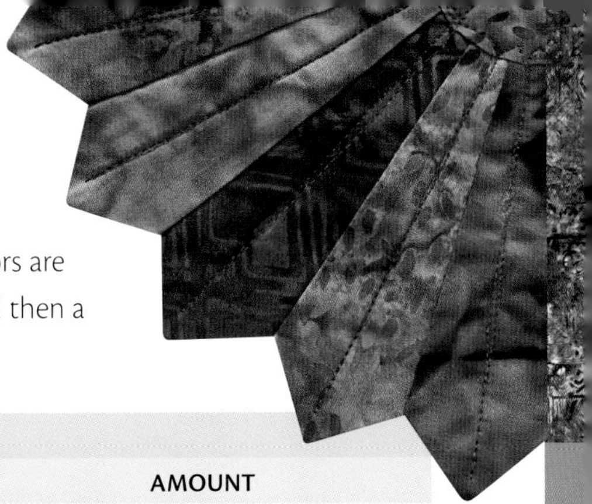

Fabric Requirements and Cutting

First, choose a border print that has at least 3 colors incorporated in the design. These colors are used in the Dresden blocks, placing 1 color in the center, surrounded by the 2nd color, and then a final ring of the 3rd color. For the blades of the Dresden, 5 fabrics are used for each color.

FARFALLE FABRIC AND SUPPLY REQUIREMENTS

MATERIALS	FOR	AMOUNT
Background fabric (light)	Blocks, side setting triangles, and corner triangles	3½ yards
5 assorted fabrics (green)	Blades for center blocks and quarter center circles	¼ yard of each fabric
5 assorted fabrics (purple)	Blades for middle ring blocks and quarter center circles	⅓ yard of each fabric
5 assorted fabrics (blue)	Blades for outer ring blocks and quarter center circles	½ yard of each fabric
Accent fabric (purple) Note: May be 1 of the 5 assorted block fabrics.	Inner border	½ yard
Medium to large multicolored print fabric	Outer border	2 yards
	Binding	⅝ yard
Backing fabric	Backing	5⅓ yards
Batting	Filler	77″ × 94″

FARFALLE CUTTING INSTRUCTIONS

FABRIC	FOR	STRIPS	SUBCUT	CIRCLES
Background fabric (light)	Blocks	Cut 14 strips 6½″ × WOF*.	Subcut 82 squares 6½″ × 6½″.	—
	Side setting triangles	Cut 2 strips 9¾″ × WOF.	Subcut 5 squares 9¾″ × 9¾″. Cut again into triangles by cutting diagonally twice. Yields 20 triangles.	—
	Corner triangles	Cut 1 strip 9⅜″ × WOF.	Subcut 2 squares 9⅜″ × 9⅜″. Cut again into triangles by cutting diagonally once. Yields 4 triangles.	
5 assorted fabrics (green)	Blades for center blocks	Cut 1 strip from each fabric 5¼″ × WOF.	Subcut 6 from each fabric using template E. (Use pressing template EE.)	—
	Quarter center circles for center blocks	—	—	Cut 6 using template L. (Use pressing template RR.) Note: May be cut from any combination of fabrics.
5 assorted fabrics (purple)	Blades for blocks in middle ring	Cut 1 strip from each fabric 5¼″ × WOF.	Subcut 24 from each fabric using template E. (Use pressing template EE.)	—
	Quarter center circles for blocks in middle ring	—	—	Cut 24 using template L. (Use pressing template RR.) Note: May be cut from any combination of fabrics.
5 assorted fabrics (blue)	Blades for blocks in outer ring	Cut 2 strips from each fabric 5¼″ × WOF.	Subcut 40 from each fabric using template E. (Use pressing template EE.)	—
	Quarter center circles for blocks in outer ring	—	—	Cut 40 using template L. (Use pressing template RR.) Note: May be cut from any combination of fabrics.
Accent fabric (purple)	Inner border	Cut 7 strips 2″ × WOF.	—	—
Medium to large multicolored print fabric	Outer border	Cut 8 strips 8″ × WOF.	—	—
	Binding	Cut 9 strips 2¼″ × WOF.	—	—

* WOF = width of fabric

Making the Dresden Blocks

1. Determine the layout of the colors for each of the 3 colorations for the Dresden blades.

Green, purple, and blue color layouts for quarter blocks

2. Follow the directions in Peaked-Top Blade, page 9, to prepare the peaked-top blades.

3. Follow the directions in Preparing Quarter Blocks and Sewing Blades onto the Quarter Block, pages 16–17, to sew the blades onto the blocks, making the following quantities: 6 green quarter squares, 24 purple quarter squares, and 40 blue quarter squares.

4. Make the quarter center circles using the directions in Sewing a Quarter Circle, page 18, in the following quantities: 6 green, 24 purple, and 40 blue.

5. Appliqué the quarter center circles in place using the stitch of your choice.

Assembling the Top

Quilt assembly diagram

1. Refer to the diagram, and sew the blocks together as diagonal rows. Press the seams for each row in opposite directions.

2. Sew the rows together. Press the seams as desired.

Inner and Outer Borders

Refer to Mitered Border Corners, page 65, for measuring and sewing borders.

Quilting

The blades have a single line of stitching down the center. An allover spiral design was quilted for the background, and a diamond grid was stitched on the border. Peggy Parsons used the shapes on the fabric as her inspiration for the quilting designs.

Abendessen Table Runner

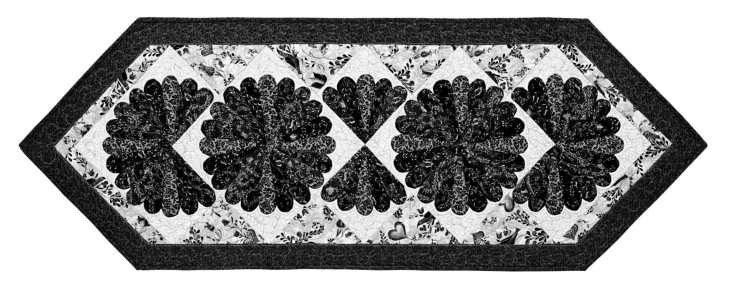

Pieced by Anelie Belden; quilted by Kathy Schmidt.

FINISHED QUARTER BLOCK: 6″ × 6″ | **FINISHED TABLE RUNNER:** 60⅜″ × 21½″ | **SKILL LEVEL 2—INTERMEDIATE**

On-point setting, curved-top blade, fractured Dresden

Abendessen: German for "dinnertime," this table runner has an on-point setting and curved-top blade, making it an intermediate project. To make it a skill level 1 project, change the blade top to a straight or peaked design.

Fabric Requirements and Cutting

The fabrics shown are from the Fraktur Fancy collection by P & B Textiles. The collection is inspired by Pennsylvania German folk art, which seems so appropriate for the Dresden design. The side setting triangles are made from a large print with a dark background. The blades and center circles are made with 5 different fabrics that are pieced on a tone-on-tone print.

ABENDESSEN TABLE RUNNER FABRIC AND SUPPLY REQUIREMENTS		
MATERIALS	**FOR**	**AMOUNT**
Background fabric (light blue tone-on-tone print)	Blocks	¾ yard
5 assorted fabrics (prints)	Blades and quarter center circles	¼ yard of each fabric
Large-print fabric (medium blue)	Side setting triangles and end strips	½ yard
Tone-on-tone fabric (medium dark burgundy)	Outer border	⅜ yard
	Binding	⅝ yard
Backing fabric	Backing	2 yards
Batting	Filler	27″ × 69″
Lightweight interfacing, 36″ wide	Lining for curved tops of blades	⅓ yard

ABENDESSEN TABLE RUNNER CUTTING INSTRUCTIONS				
FABRIC	**FOR**	**STRIPS**	**SUBCUT**	**CIRCLES**
Background fabric (light blue tone-on-tone print)	Blocks	Cut 3 strips 6½″ × WOF*.	Subcut 16 squares 6½″ × 6½″.	—
5 assorted fabrics (prints)	Blades	Cut 1 strip from each fabric 5¼″ wide × WOF.	Subcut 16 blades from each fabric using template E. (Use pressing template HH.)	—
	Quarter center circles	—	—	Cut 16 using template L. (Use pressing template RR.) Note: May be cut from any combination of fabrics.
Large-print fabric (medium blue)	Side setting triangles	Cut 1 strip 9¾″ × WOF.	Subcut 2 squares 9¾″ × 9¾″. Cut again into triangles by cutting diagonally twice. Yields 8 triangles.	—
	End strips	Cut 2 strips 2″ × WOF.	—	—
Tone-on-tone fabric (medium dark burgundy)	Outer border	Cut 4 strips 2½″ × WOF.	—	—
	Binding	Cut bias strips 2½″ wide. Piece to make a strip approximately 185″ long.	—	—
Lightweight interfacing	Lining for curved tops of blades	Cut 6 strips 1½″ × WOF.	—	Subcut 80 using template AAA. (Use pressing template HH.)

* WOF = width of fabric

Making the Dresden Blocks

1. Determine the layout of the colors for the Dresden blades.

2. Follow the directions in Curved-Top Blade, page 11, to prepare the curved-top blades, making 80 blades.

3. Follow the directions in Preparing Quarter Blocks and Sewing Blades onto the Quarter Block, pages 16–17, to sew the blades onto the blocks, making 16 quarter blocks.

Adding the Quarter Center Circles

1. Make the quarter center circles using the directions in Sewing a Quarter Circle, page 18, making a total of 16. Note: Each quarter block has a different color quarter center circle.

2. Pin or glue in place. Stitch around them as desired.

Assembling the Top

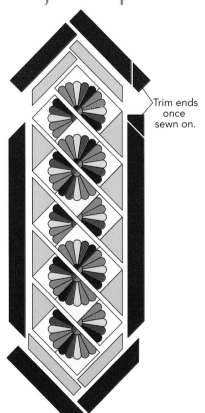

Trim ends once sewn on.

Assembly diagram

⊙ LAYOUT TIP

You are less likely to make a mistake if you lay the entire table runner out on a design wall to see how the blocks and side setting triangles go together.

1. Begin by sewing the blocks and side setting triangles into diagonal rows, pressing seams from row to row in opposite directions.

2. Sew the rows together. Pin at the intersections to be sure the seams match. Press the seams in one direction. Once all the rows are sewn together, press well and trim, leaving ¼" from the seam intersection for seam allowance.

3. Sew the large-print end strips to each angled side of the ends of the table runner. Trim the excess ends off.

Border

1. Sew the side borders on first. Press the seams toward the border. Trim.

2. Sew the end border pieces on the remaining 4 sides. Trim. Press the seams toward the border.

⊙ SETTING TIP

If you prefer a squared-off end, add 2 corner triangles to each end.

Quilting

The tole-painting design of the fabric inspired Kathy Schmidt to quilt using feathering for the blades, side-setting triangles, and border. The background is quilted fairly densely with a curvy teardrop design.

Gallery of Quilts
with On-Point Settings

Ivory Blade; 90″ × 71″;
curved-top blade, small block
Pieced and quilted by Carol Machado.

Winterberries Table Runner; 18″ × 46″;
peaked-top blade, small block
Pieced by Patty Hubbard; quilted by Kathy Schmidt.

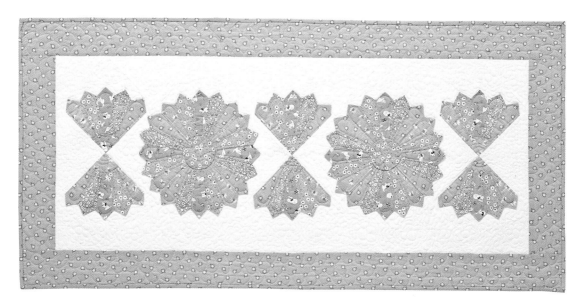

Grandma's Dresden Table Runner; 47″ × 22½″;
peaked-top blade, small block
Pieced by Lola Thomas; quilted by Anelie Belden.

Dresden Done Royal

Pieced and quilted by Beverly Kelly Swift.

FINISHED QUARTER BLOCK: 9˝ × 9˝ | FINISHED QUILT: 70½˝ × 70½˝ | SKILL LEVEL 2—INTERMEDIATE

Straight sashed setting, split peaked-top blade, continuous Dresden

This quilt is quite striking, yet not difficult to make. The peaked-top construction is fairly simple, and the technique for splitting the blade is easier than it looks. The Dresden blades are separated with sashing, which allows a bit of forgiveness in matching the sides of the block.

Fabric Requirements and Cutting

The main background fabric should be a medium to large multicolored print. The print used here has a lot of movement and a variety of colors from which to draw. Choose 5 colors from the main fabric as the blades. One half of the blade is a darker shade of the color, and the other half is a lighter shade, adding dimension to the design. The blades are put on a background with high contrast, so the Dresden design is sharp and distinct.

DRESDEN DONE ROYAL FABRIC AND SUPPLY REQUIREMENTS		
MATERIALS	**FOR**	**AMOUNT**
Dark background fabric (medium to large multi-colored print)	Blocks, border blocks, quarter center circles, and cornerstones	2⅛ yards
Light background fabric (tone-on-tone print)	Dresden blocks	1¾ yards
5 darker fabrics (small prints)	Dark side of blades and cornerstones	⅜ yard each fabric
5 lighter fabrics (small prints)	Lighter side of blades and cornerstones	⅜ yard each fabric
Dark fabric (tone-on-tone print)	Sashing	1¼ yards
	Binding	⅝ yard
Backing fabric	Backing	4½ yards
Batting	Filler	78″ × 78″

DRESDEN DONE ROYAL CUTTING INSTRUCTIONS				
FABRIC	**FOR**	**STRIPS**	**SUBCUT**	**CIRCLES**
Dark background fabric (medium to large multicolored print)	Blocks	Cut 3 strips 9½″ × WOF*.	Subcut 12 squares 9½″ × 9½″.	—
	Border blocks, corner blocks	Cut 7 strip 5″ × WOF.	Subcut 24 rectangles 9½″ × 5″ and 4 squares 5″ × 5″.	—
	Cornerstones	Cut 1 strip 1½″ × WOF.	Subcut 25 squares 1½″ × 1½″.	—
	Quarter center circles	Cut 2 strips 2¼″ × WOF.	—	Subcut 24 using template M. (Use pressing template SS.)
Light background fabric (tone-on-tone print)	Dresden blocks	Cut 6 strips 9½″ × WOF.	Subcut 24 squares 9½″ × 9½″.	—
5 darker fabrics (small prints)	Dark side of blades	Cut 3 strips 3″ × WOF from each fabric.	Piece together with a lighter fabric, then subcut 24 from each fabric pair using template F. (Use pressing template FF.)	—
	Cornerstones	Cut 1 strip 1½″ × WOF.	Subcut 12 squares 1½″ × 1½″.	—
5 lighter fabrics (small prints)	Lighter side of blades	Cut 3 strips 3″ × WOF from each fabric.	Piece together with a darker fabric, then subcut 24 from each fabric pair using template F. (Use pressing template FF.)	—
	Cornerstones	Cut 1 strip 1½″ × WOF.	Subcut 12 squares 1½″ × 1½″.	—
Dark fabric (tone-on-tone print)	Sashing	Cut 25 strips 1½″ × WOF.	Subcut 84 strips, 1½″ × 9½″ and 28 strips, 1½″ × 5″.	—
	Binding	Cut 8 strips 2¼″ × WOF.	—	—

* WOF = width of fabric

Making the Dresden Blocks

Sewing the Split Blades

All of the blocks can be the same fabrication, or they can have a random scrappy look. Begin by creating the strip pieces for the blades.

Using the 3″ strips of dark fabric and a lighter fabric of the same color, make 120 split peaked-top blades following the directions in Making Split Peaked-Top Blades, page 9.

Sewing Blades onto the Quarter Blocks

1. Determine the layout of the colors for the Dresden quarter blocks. Make 24 scrappy blocks or 24 blocks all using the same layout.

2. Follow the directions in Preparing Quarter Blocks and Sewing Blades onto the Quarter Block, pages 16–17, to sew the blades onto the blocks.

3. Prepare the quarter center circles according to the directions in Sewing a Quarter Circle, page 18.

4. Appliqué them onto the squares, and stitch the tops of the blades in place using the stitching method of your choice.

Assembling the Top

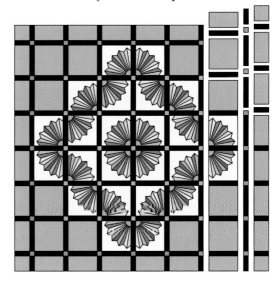

Quilt assembly diagram

1. Using a design wall, lay the quilt out as shown in the quilt assembly diagram. Note: Dark background fabric was used for the 25 interior cornerstones. The perimeter cornerstones are a mix of the dark and light blade fabrics.

2. Referring to the diagram, sew each row together, pressing the seams toward the sashing. Note: The border sections are incorporated while piecing the top together.

3. Sew the rows to each other, pinning first at each seam intersection to ensure that they will align.

Quilting

The lighter Dresden blocks were quilted using a dense loopy background design. The same design was repeated on the multiprint blocks, but in a larger scale. The blades and quarter center circles were stitched ¼″ from the outer edges, allowing them to rise up a little. The sashing has no quilting but was stitched in the ditch on all sides, giving it a clean, crisp look.

Gypsy Summer

Pieced by Anelie Belden; quilted by Kathy Schmidt.

FINISHED BLOCK: 12″ × 12″ | FINISHED QUILT: 52½″ × 52½″ | SKILL LEVEL 2—INTERMEDIATE

Straight sashed setting, three-sided and peaked-top blades, fractured Dresden

The setting of the quarter Dresden blocks gives the illusion of curved lines in this quilt. It uses small, medium, and large blades, and if desired, the design can be made without the sashing.

Fabric Requirements and Cutting

Gypsy Summer uses a fabric collection, *Maypole*, designed by April Cornell and produced by Moda. The variety of prints and colors makes the quilt burst with cheer. The center Dresden is fussy cut using a striped floral print.

GYPSY SUMMER FABRIC AND SUPPLY REQUIREMENTS		
MATERIALS	**FOR**	**AMOUNT**
Dark pink background fabric (tone-on-tone print)	Center block and center triangles (star points)	½ yard
Light yellow background fabric (tone-on-tone print)	Large background squares	⅞ yard
Light yellow background fabric (medium/large print)	Medium background squares	⅜ yard
Medium blue background fabric (medium print)	Triangles	¼ yard
Dark blue background fabric (medium print)	Small triangles on border	½ yard
Medium green background fabric (medium print)	Border rectangles and corner squares	½ yard
Medium green background fabric (tone-on-tone print)	Large triangles on border and cornerstones	⅝ yard
5 fabrics (small prints)	Medium blades	¼ yard of each fabric
5 fabrics (large print)	Large blades and full center circle	⅓ yard of each fabric
Medium multicolor print fabric	Center full Dresden	⅓–½ yard Note: 20 repeats of the print are needed to cut blades for the center Dresden.
Dark red fabric (tone-on-tone print)	Sashing	½ yard
	Binding	½ yard
Light green fabric (tone-on-tone print)	Quarter center circles	⅛ yard
Backing fabric	Backing	3½ yards
Batting	Filler	60″ × 60″

GYPSY SUMMER CUTTING INSTRUCTIONS				
FABRIC	**FOR**	**STRIPS**	**SUBCUT**	**CIRCLES**
Dark pink background fabric (tone-on-tone print)	Center block	Cut 1 strip 6½″ × WOF*.	Subcut 4 squares 6½″ × 6½″.	—
	Center triangles (star points)	Cut 1 strip 6⅞″ × WOF.	Subcut 4 squares 6⅞″ × 6⅞″. Subcut again diagonally into 8 triangles.	—
Light yellow background fabric (tone-on-tone print)	Large background squares	Cut 2 strips 12½″ × WOF.	Subcut 4 squares 12½″ × 12½″.	—
Light yellow background fabric (medium/large print)	Medium background squares	Cut 1 strip 9″ × WOF.	Subcut 4 squares 9″ × 9″.	—
Medium blue background fabric (medium print)	Interior triangles	Cut 1 strip 6⅞″ × WOF.	Subcut 4 squares 6⅞″ × 6⅞″. Subcut again diagonally into 8 triangles.	
Dark blue background fabric (medium print)	Small triangles on border	Cut 2 strips 6⅞″ × WOF.	Subcut 8 squares 6⅞″ × 6⅞″. Subcut again diagonally into 16 triangles.	—
Medium green background fabric (medium print)	Border rectangles and corner squares	Cut 2 strips 6½″ × WOF.	Subcut 4 rectangles 6½″ × 12½″ and 4 squares 6½″ × 6½″.	—

FABRIC	FOR	STRIPS	SUBCUT	CIRCLES
Medium green background fabric (tone-on-tone print)	Large triangles on border	Cut 1 strip 13¼" × WOF.	Subcut 2 squares 13¼" × 13¼". Cut again twice diagonally into 8 triangles.	—
	Cornerstones	Cut 1 strip 1½" × WOF.	Subcut 16 squares 1½" × 1½".	—
5 fabrics (small prints)	Medium blades	Cut 1 strip 6½" × WOF from each fabric.	Subcut 4 blades of each fabric using template B. (Use pressing template XX.) Note: This is the straight-top template but the blades will be constructed with a peaked top.	—
5 fabrics (large prints)	Large blades	Cut 1 strip 9⅞" × WOF from each fabric.	Subcut 4 blades of each fabric using template G. (Use pressing template MM.)	—
Medium multicolor print fabric	Center full Dresden	—	Fussy cut 20 blades using template E. (Use pressing template KK.)	—
	Full center circle	—	—	Cut and press 1 using template XX.
Dark red fabric (tone-on-tone print)	Sashing	Cut 11 strips 1½" wide × WOF.	Subcut 16 strips 1½" × 6½" and 24 strips 1½" × 12½".	—
	Binding	Cut 6 strips 2¼" wide × WOF.	—	—
Light green fabric (tone-on-tone print)	Quarter center circles	—	—	Cut 4 using template N. (Use pressing template TT.) Cut 4 using template M. (Use pressing template SS.)

* WOF = width of fabric

● Fussy-Cutting Directions

To make 1 full Dresden with the same design repeated on each blade, choose a part of the design that can be cut 20 times. Make a template of the three-sided blade. Lay it on top of the fabric, and draw the design onto the template, which will be used as a guide when cutting all of the blades. Lay the template on the fabric, place an acrylic ruler next to it, and cut with a rotary cutter.

Fussy-cut with template.

Small Full Center Block

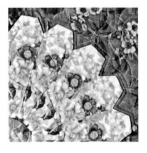

1. The center block is made of 4 quarter blocks with fussy-cut blades. Follow the directions in Three-Sided-Top Blade, page 10, to make the three-sided blades.

2. Follow the directions in Preparing Quarter Blocks and Sewing Blades onto the Quarter Block, pages 16–17, to sew the blades onto the blocks. Make 4 blocks.

3. Sew the 4 blocks together to make a full Dresden. Prepare a center circle as directed in Sewing a Full Center Circle, page 18. Appliqué the center circle in place.

Medium Quarter Dresden Blocks

1. Determine the layout of the colors for the Dresden quarter blocks. Follow the directions in Peaked-Top Blade, page 9, to make the peaked-top blades.

2. Follow the directions in Preparing Quarter Blocks and Sewing Blades onto the Quarter Block, pages 16–17, to sew the blades onto the blocks. Make 4 blocks, all using the same layout.

3. Prepare the quarter center circles as directed in Sewing a Quarter Circle, page 18. Appliqué them onto the squares, and stitch the tops of the blades down using the stitching method of your choice.

4. Sew 2 of the side triangles onto adjoining sides of each of the quarter Dresden blocks. Press the seams toward the triangles.

5. Sew the remaining 2 side triangles onto the remaining sides of each of the quarter Dresden blocks. Press the seams toward the triangles. The block should measure 12½″.

Sew side triangles onto Dresden block.

Large Quarter Dresden Blocks

1. Determine the layout of the colors for the Dresden quarter blocks.

2. Follow the directions in Three-Sided-Top Blade, page 10, to make the three-sided top blades.

3. Follow the directions in Preparing Quarter Blocks and Sewing Blades onto the Quarter Block, pages 16–17, to sew the blades onto the blocks. Make 4 blocks, all using the same layout.

4. Prepare the quarter center circles as directed in Sewing a Quarter Circle, page 18. Appliqué them onto the squares, and stitch the tops of the blades down using the stitching method of your choice.

Assembling the Top

Quilt assembly diagram

1. Using a design wall, lay the quilt out as in the project photo, page 60, and the assembly diagram.

2. Referring to the diagram, sew each row together, pressing the seams toward the sashing. Note: The border sections are incorporated while piecing the top together.

3. Sew the rows to each other, pinning at each seam intersection to ensure alignment.

Quilting

Kathy Schmidt quilted the Dresden blades using a simple echo design. The background was quilted a bit more densely using the cherries, floral, and leaf designs printed on the fabric. The outer blocks have a grid pattern and other linear designs.

Gallery of Quilts with Sashed Settings

Dots of Fun; 67½″ × 67½″;
split blades, peaked-top blade, medium block
Pieced and quilted by Carol Machado.

Window Lace; 55″ × 69″;
three-sided top, small block
Pieced by Jan Ramsey; quilted by Chris Zeterberg.

Chick Happens; 33″ × 33″;
three-sided top, medium block
Pieced and quilted by Shannon Freeman.

General Quilt Finishing Instructions

Standard Borders—No-Measure Method

Borders can add both size and beauty to a quilt top. They also provide a frame around the quilt, giving the top a finished look. Inner borders can add an accent color or a color separation between the quilt top and the outer border. To keep the border in balance with the quilt, a rule of thumb is that the total width of all borders should not be wider than the blocks in the top.

One of the challenges when putting on the borders is that they may get stretched out of shape. It is important to sew the correct length on each side *and* to be sure the sides are the same length as each other so the quilt will be flat. This is especially true if the quilt will be hanging on a wall or shown in a quilt show.

One method of determining the length needed for borders is to measure the middle of the quilt, but I find this can be inaccurate and frustrating. The following alternate method is one that is successful for me and easy for those who are mathematically challenged.

Determining the Border Length

1. Fold the quilt in half and then in half again (quarters).

2. Place the quilt on a cutting mat, with the raw edge that will join the border on a line, being careful that it is nice and straight; the other raw-edge side should also be straight.

4. Take the border lengths, and fold them in half.

5. Lay a folded border directly below the quilt top, lining up the fold and the straight edge to the quilt top.

6. Once everything is aligned, trim away the extra border length. Repeat for the second border length.

7. Once the borders are sewn on, repeat the process for the remaining 2 sides.

Fold quilt into quarters. Align folded border with folded quilt. Cut border.

Mitered Border Corners

Use the following formula to determine the length the borders need to be:

1. Measure the length of the quilt side the border is being sewn onto.

2. Add twice the width of the border being sewn onto each side of the quilt (border width times 2).

3. Add a few inches for safety.

◎ MULTIPLE-BORDER TIP

When there are multiple borders on a quilt, sew the strips together and treat the pieced borders as one.

Sewing the Border onto the Quilt

1. Find the center of the border along the long side; mark or pin.

2. Lay the border on a table, face up, as flat as possible.

3. Find the center of the side edge of the quilt.

4. Lay the quilt face down on top of the border, matching the center markings. Pin it in place.

5. Sew the border on, starting and stopping ¼" from the corners of the quilt. Sew with the back of the quilt facing up, so you can see the corners of the quilt.

Do not press the seam at this time. You will press after the mitered corner is sewn. Repeat the previous steps for the three remaining sides, leaving the borders hanging free at each corner.

Preparing to Sew the Mitered Corners

1. Once all 4 borders are sewn on, lay the quilt on the table face down, with the wrong side facing up.

2. Choose the corner you will do first. Pick up the raw edges of the seams where the border is sewn onto the quilt top. Fold the quilt into a triangle, and sandwich it between the borders. Pin through the layers to hold the border in place.

Pick up quilt to sew mitered corners.

Marking the Start of the Mitered Seam

1. Mark just to the right (hairline) of the fold of the quilt top on the border.

2. Mark the ¼″ seamline.

You will begin stitching the mitered seam where the 2 lines cross.

Mark start of mitered corner.

Marking the Mitered Seamline

You will need a ruler with a 45° angle marked on it.

1. Lay the quilt on a cutting mat, lining up the straight edges on the lines of the mat. This will help to keep the edges at the proper angles. Note: The quilt is still folded as in the previous steps.

2. Put the ruler on the borders with the 45° angle along the raw edge of the border.

3. Slide the ruler along the border until the angle crosses the marked point where the mitered seam will begin. Double-check that the ruler is straight with the border's raw edge and that it lines up where the mitered seam will begin.

4. Using a fabric-marking tool, draw the line in place.

5. Pin along the line to hold it in place before sewing. Note: If you have multiple borders that were sewn together, align the seams so they will match when sewn.

6. Sew along the line, being sure not to catch the fold of the quilt.

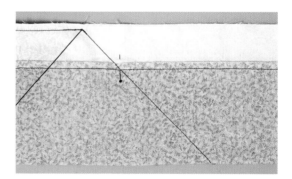

Pin and sew.

Finishing

1. Unpin and open the mitered corner. Examine it to see if it lies nicely.

2. Once you are happy with the seam, trim away the excess border fabric to about a ½″ seam allowance.

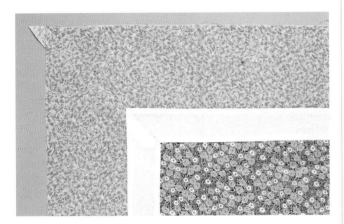

Finish mitered corners.

3. Press the seam in the direction that is most successful: open, both sides to the left, or both to the right.

Backing

Through the years, I have had many experiences with the backing of my quilts. At first, I purchased fabric for the backing. This was expensive, and sometimes when the quilt was finished, I did not like the backing I had chosen.

Another option is to wait until the quilt top is complete and then choose the backing. This can be a problem, especially if it takes years to finish the quilt top; fabrics may have changed so much that it's difficult to find a match.

My solution to this is to purchase an ample amount of each fabric for the piecing of the top. This ensures that there is enough fabric even if cutting errors are made. If by some miracle no errors occur, there should be plenty of fabric left, which then can be used to piece the backing. You can purchase more fabric if needed, but often the leftovers are sufficient. This makes for good use of fabric scraps and makes a creative, interesting back. If some of the blocks made for the top are not the correct size or are not perfect, they, too, can become part of the back. Using these blocks as a label or piecing a label into the back works too.

Pieced backing and label of *Polka Dot Daze*

Binding

Binding is usually cut on the crosswise grain, 2¼″ wide by the width of the fabric. The exception to this is for quilts that have a shaped or curved edge. For this, the binding should be cut on the bias, because bias has a stretch to it; I recommend cutting on the bias 2½″ wide.

Piecing the Binding Strips

When piecing, use a diagonal seam as shown to make 1 strip long enough to go around the entire quilt. Using a diagonal seam eliminates a bulky seam when folding.

1. Lay the ends on top of each other, with right sides together. The ends should extend past the sides of the fabric. This allows you to see exactly where the fabrics intersect.

2. Draw a line diagonally where the fabrics cross. This line MUST be exactly from intersection to intersection.

3. Sew the lengths together on the drawn line. Fold the binding over to see if the seam intersected correctly. If it's correct, trim away to leave a ¼″ seam allowance, and press open.

4. Press the pieced strip in half lengthwise, with wrong sides together.

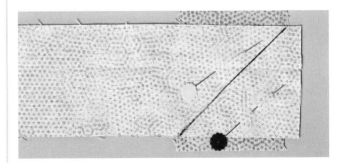

Piece binding strips.

Sewing the Binding onto the Quilt

1. Lay the binding onto the edge of the front of the quilt, lining up the raw edges. Start on a side, not at a corner; leave an unsewn tail length of about 6″ at the beginning.

2. Stop ¼″ from the corner; this is very important for the corner to lie correctly.

Stop ¼″ from corner.

Corner Fold

1. Fold the binding back, away from the direction it will be going, creating a mitered corner. Important: The binding needs to be straight back to get a good corner. It is helpful to lay the quilt's edge along the line on a cutting board to ensure that it is straight.

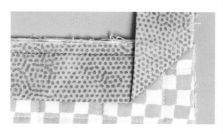

Fold binding back.

2. Fold the binding forward in the direction it will be going. Keep the fold at the raw edge of the quilt.

3. Start sewing at the folded edge. Check that the corner will fold over to the other side correctly; repeat at each corner.

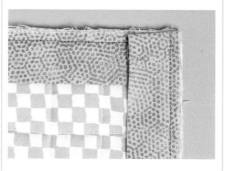

Fold binding forward; stitch.

Ending the Binding

1. Unfold the end, and open it flat onto the quilt.

2. Fold one end at a bias angle, and cut along the fold.

Unfold and cut binding end.

3. With the other end opened and flat, draw the cut bias angle onto the uncut end.

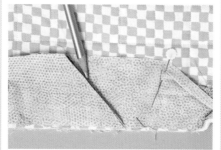

4. Add ½″ to the drawn line on the uncut end, and cut along this line.

5. Bring both ends together with right sides facing each other. Matching the angles, align the corners ¼″ from the cut edges. Sew with a ¼″ seam allowance along the angle lines.

Sew seam.

6. Press the seams in one direction. The binding should then lie flat on the quilt; sew using a ¼″ seam.

Finish end of binding.

7. Once the binding is attached and stitched to the front of the quilt, roll the binding to the back, and stitch with an invisible hand appliqué stitch (see Dresden Stitches, page 12).

Adding a Hanging Sleeve

When deciding the width of the sleeve, consider the size of the rod you will use to hang the quilt. If you are planning to enter the quilt into a show, check to see if there are size requirements for the sleeve width. The directions below are for a standard sleeve that works for most quilts.

1. As a standard measurement, cut a strip 9" wide by the width of the finished quilt. Add a few inches to the width for hems.

2. Hem the short ends. The finished sleeve should fit about 1" in from the side edges of the quilt.

3. Sew the raw edges together with *wrong* sides together. Roll the sleeve so the seam is toward the back of the sleeve, and place it against the back of the quilt.

4. Hand stitch the sleeve in place along the upper and lower edges.

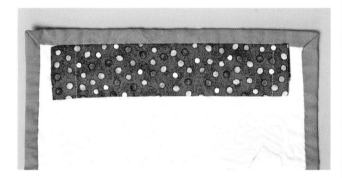

Finished sleeve

Labeling Your Quilt

It is so important to make a label that tells future generations something about the quilt. At a minimum, you should include the following information:

- Who made and quilted the quilt

- The date the quilt was made

- The name of the quilt pattern

- Any other information that you would like to include

Create the label by stitching the information by hand or machine or by writing it with a permanent fabric-marking pen.

Label of *Farfalle*

Dresden Templates

Cutting, Pressing, and Placement Templates

Three types of templates are used when making a Dresden block: cutting, pressing, and placement. Using templates carefully provides a high degree of accuracy so that your Dresden designs will be exact in size and fit together perfectly.

The templates for the Dresden designs in this book can be traced onto freezer paper or template plastic from the patterns found on the pullout. Trace the template from the page onto the selected template material using a fine-tip Sharpie pen. Rather than drawing the lines freehand, use a ruler for straight lines and a compass for any curved edges. After cutting out the template, always check it against the drawing to ensure that the shape has not been distorted.

Cutting Templates

The cutting templates are used as patterns for the blades and the center circles of the Dresden design. First, decide on the material you prefer for the templates, and then follow the directions above for tracing or copying the template.

Pressing Templates

Pressing templates are used to ensure consistent and accurate pressing of the tops of the blades. The templates can be made from freezer paper or Mylar template plastic. Quilter's Freezer Paper Sheets are a new product available for printing directly onto freezer paper. These 8½″ × 11″ pages of freezer paper will go through most home computer printers, letting you print, instead of trace, the templates.

There are two ways to make pressing templates.

- Make the template and lay it on the blade, then shape the top by folding fabric over it (straight and three-sided blades), or tuck inside the top to shape the blade (peaked-top or curved-top blades), and press well.

- Lay the template on the ironing board, or draw it onto a piece of preshrunk muslin. Then lay the blade on top of the template shape, and use it as a guide. This works best for the peaked top.

Placement Template

The placement templates are guides used for placing the blades in the correct position on the blocks. Make the templates according to the directions, and see Preparing Quarter Blocks and Sewing Blades onto the Quarter Block, pages 16–17, for placement instructions. A quick and accurate method of making transparent placement templates is to have your local copy center copy them onto clear plastic transparency film, such as that used for overhead projectors. You can then simply cut them out using craft scissors.

About the Author

After enjoying a San Francisco-based career in the fashion industry, Anelie moved with her family to the rural town of Volcano, California. Here she and her husband, Kevin, settled and raised their three children, Joshua, Amilia, and Christopher. During these years, Anelie had time to use her sewing background and learned to quilt. She was a quick study and soon owned a quilt store and was teaching others.

Before long, Anelie began designing quilts and producing quilt patterns. She began organizing quilt retreats, writing a block-of-the-month series for the local paper, and appearing on the local television station, educating the community about quilts.

©2008 by Carolyn Fox, www.angier-fox.com

For more information about Anelie, visit her website at www.anelie.com

Resources

For a list of other fine books from C&T Publishing, visit our website to view our catalog online:

C&T PUBLISHING, INC.
P.O. Box 1456
Lafayette, CA 94549
(800) 284-1114
Email: ctinfo@ctpub.com
Website: www.ctpub.com

C&T Publishing's professional photography services are now available to the public.
Visit us at www.ctmediaservices.com.

For quilting supplies:

COTTON PATCH
1025 Brown Ave.
Lafayette, CA 94549
Store: (925) 284-1177
Mail order: (925) 283-7883
Email: CottonPa@aol.com
Website: www.quiltusa.com

Note:

Fabrics used in the quilts shown may not be currently available, as fabric manufacturers keep most fabrics in print for only a short time.

Check the following fabric company websites to find local independent quilt shops near you that carry their fabrics.

Moda Fabrics, www.unitednotions.com

P&B Textiles, www.pbtex.com

Michael Miller Fabrics, www.michaelmillerfabrics.com

Machine quilting like that featured on the quilts in this book is offered by the following:

Cheryl Ehlman, cehlman@volcano.net

Chris Zeterberg, countrypatchwork@amadorca.com

Peggy Parsons, pandptasha@earthlink.net

Susan Huntington, creativequilter@juno.com

Any of the tools, supplies, and templates mentioned in the book can be purchased by visiting Anelie's website at www.anelie.com.

Great Titles
from C&T PUBLISHING

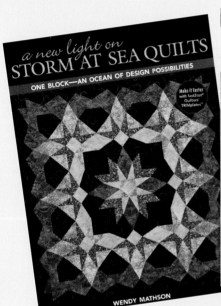

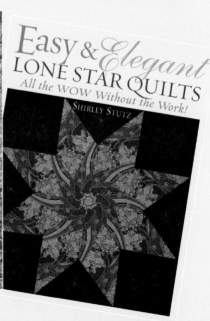